Crowell Publications in History

Advi for American History

Ubbeloh

The ers
th

MOU JEPH

The Crowell American History Series
JOHN HOPE FRANKLIN & ABRAHAM S. EISENSTADT, *Editors*

The American Mind in the Mid-Nineteenth Century
IRVING H. BARTLETT
Parties and Politics in the Early Republic, 1789-1815
MORTON BORDEN
America in the Twenties
PAUL A. CARTER
The New Deal
PAUL K. CONKIN
The Ferment of Reform, 1830-1860
C. S. GRIFFIN
The American Colonies and the British Empire,
    1607-1763
CARL UBBELOHDE
From Isolation to War, 1931-1941
JOHN E. WILTZ

Carl Ubbelohde
CASE WESTERN RESERVE UNIVERSITY

The American Colonies and the British Empire, 1607-1763

Thomas Y. Crowell Company
NEW YORK
ESTABLISHED 1834

For Susan, Nell, Libby, and Kate

Library of Congress Catalog Card Number: 68–13389

Series design by Judith Woracek Barry

Manufactured in the United States of America

EDITORS' FOREWORD

It is a commonplace that each age writes its own history, for the reason that man sees the past in the foreshortened perspective of his own experience. This has certainly been true of the writing of American history. The purpose of our historical writing remains constant: to offer us a more certain sense of where we are going by indicating the road we have taken in getting there. But it is precisely because our own generation is redefining its direction, the way other generations have redefined theirs before us, that the substance of our historical writing is changing. We are thinking anew of our direction because of our newer values and premises, our newer sense of how we can best fulfill the goals of our society, our newer outlook on the meaning of American life. Thus, the vitality of the present inspires the vitality of our writing about the past.

It is the plan of the *Crowell American History Series* to offer the reader a survey of the point of arrival of recent scholarship on the central themes and problems of American history. The scholars we have invited to do the respective volumes of the series are younger individuals whose monographs have been well received by their peers and who have demonstrated their mastery of the subjects on which they are writing. The author of each volume has undertaken to present a summation of the principal lines of discussion that historians of a particular subject have been pursuing. However, he has not written a mere digest of historical literature. The author has been concerned to offer the reader a sufficient factual and narrative account to help him perceive the larger dimensions of the subject. Each author, moreover, has arrived at his own conclusions about those aspects of his subject that have been matters of difference and contro- versy. In effect, he has written not only about where the subject stands in historiography but also about where he himself stands on the subject. And each volume concludes with an extensive critical essay on authorities.

The books in this series are designed for use in the basic course in American history, although they could be used, with great benefit, in advanced courses as well. Such a series has a particular utility in times such as these, when the traditional format of our American history courses is being altered to accommodate a greater diversity of texts and reading materials. The series offers a number of distinct advantages. It extends and deepens the dimensions of course work in American history. In proceeding beyond the confines of the traditional textbook, it makes clear that the study of our past is, more than the student might otherwise infer, at once complex, sophisticated, and pro- found. It presents American history as a subject of continuing vitality and fresh investigation. The work of experts in their respective fields, it opens up to the student the rich findings of historical inquiry. It invites the student to join with his older and more experienced colleagues in pondering anew the major themes and problems of our past. It challenges the student to participate actively in exploring American history and to seek out its wider reaches on his own.

John Hope Franklin
Abraham S. Eisenstadt

CONTENTS

ONE

Building an Empire

There were American colonies, created by English people, before there was a British Empire. After a series of ill-fated attempts to sustain an English settlement in the Western Hemisphere during the sixteenth century, the tiny group of settlers dispatched by the Virginia Company to the shores of the Chesapeake achieved historic distinction as the planters of the first permanent English colony in the New World. The year was 1607. In the course of the next four decades, for a variety of reasons, other Englishmen migrated to American shores. By the middle of the century, transplanted Englishmen were grouped in a cluster of communities in New England; Virginia had been joined in the Chesapeake area by the Calvert proprietary province of Maryland; Englishmen had developed

I

plantations on islands in the Caribbean. But there was, as of 1650, no empire, for these colonies had been conceived, born, and were struggling with their childhood problems without general supervision from the homeland and without official blueprints charting their future destinies.

The British Empire was created in the second half of the seventeenth century. It was born during the years of the Interregnum, while the Stuart family was temporarily driven from the throne of England. It was nurtured during the era called the Restoration and brought into basic maturity during the closing years of the century. It began as an economic concept, erected upon the core idea of tying the trade lanes of the miscellaneous English overseas possessions into a mercantile network for sustaining national strength. But economic regulation almost inevitably brought increased awareness of, and interest in, political and constitutional relationships, and ideas of uniformity and consolidation of control soon became imperial goals. The drive for conformity reflected additional interests after England and her colonies embarked on the series of military struggles against France, and later Spain as well, along with their New World empires.

By the early years of the eighteenth century, the basic structure of the first British Empire (of which the mainland American colonies were only one part) had been shaped. The patterns which had been evolved would remain largely unmodified during the next six decades. Of course, from time to time during those years minor alterations were needed to satisfy specific interests or elements on one or both sides of the ocean. Sometimes the patterns were slightly shifted to accommodate newer developments. But generally, imperfect and disarranged though the patterns might have appeared then and sometimes appear now, it was not until after 1763 that major (and in Americans' eyes, unconstitutional) changes precipitated the crisis of the American Revolution.

The voluminous details contained in the extant records of the first century and a half of European life in the American wilderness, including at times distressingly contradictory evidence concerning motivations and beliefs, tend to obscure the outlines of the pattern of imperial relationships. Historians have not always agreed upon the shape or dimensions of the pattern; they have often disagreed even more sharply on the relative consequences of them. Some scholars are even inclined to argue that the very concept of empire exists more fully in the minds and imaginations of present-day historians, attempting to find orderly systems in past ages, than it ever did in the minds of Englishmen or Americans in the seventeenth and eighteenth centuries. What makes the problem of assessing the history of the American colonies in the British Empire doubly difficult is the fact that, in time, the colonies ceased to be colonies. Having established themselves as independent states and joining together to fashion a republican federation, the Revolutionary generation justified, in part, its actions on the benefits to come from separation from the Empire.

Naturally, then, the men of the young Republic who wrote the earliest histories of the colonial experience to create a heritage and tradition for their new nation emphasized the local, colonial part of the Empire. The virtues of pilgrims seeking religious freedoms on the shores of the new continent, the values of democratically contrived town meetings and representative assemblies—these were the staples of the earliest American colonial history. The British Empire, with its restrictions and regulations stifling freedoms and opportunities for settlers, was a horrible handicap, a horrendous hurdle the brave American pioneers encountered along the road to freedom. George Bancroft used several volumes of his *History of the United States of America* (1834–1874) to explain it. The American colonists had been virtuous; the British full of vice, for in Europe "it was a period of corruption. . . . It would have been very easy for the British government to have conciliated affection and respect . . . but the avidity of the persons holding office was constant and too strong." Especially at fault was the "mercantilist restrictive system . . . the superstition of that age. Capitalists worshipped it; statesmen were overawed by it; philosophers dared not question it." "All questions on colonial liberty and affairs were decided from the point of view of English commerce and the interests of the great landholders." But "the system of trade and navigation, being founded in selfish injustice, was doomed . . . to expire," for "popular liberty had thriven vigorously" in the colonies, "like the tree by the rivers of water, that grows in the night-time. . . ."

Such history was American colonial history, not British imperial history. It was written by Americans, for Americans. It satisfied the people of a relatively isolated, emerging nation whose citizens believed in their unique destiny and desired an historical narrative to provide a heritage consistent with that destiny. For a hundred years after the creation of the United States as a sovereign nation its history of its origins was cast in such forms.

The last years of the nineteenth century and the opening decades of the present century brought a change. The older history might satisfy the amateur historian; it might have its uses in grammar-school textbooks and Fourth of July celebrations. But there had now come into prominence a new breed of historical scholars. These "new men" held an ideal of objectively reporting past events that led them to fear interjection of personal or national prejudices into their history. Modeled after the "scientific" historians of Germany, trained in the seminars of the new graduate schools, working with tools of unmatched caliber and dedicated to a depth of scholarship previously unknown, they embarked upon a quest which radically altered the contours of American colonial history.

These historians argued for a fresh start in the study of America's origins. They spoke for colonial history that was unimpassioned by patriotic prejudice, anti-British inclinations, or viewed only through the window of the American Revolution. Scholars such as Herbert L. Osgood, Charles M. Andrews, George L. Beer, and their disciples studied the first British Empire, particularly as it was developed and matured in relation to the mainland American colonies. They avidly sought out and recorded the history of the agencies of empire; they analyzed theories of imperial control; they came to a sympathetic understanding of the difficulties of imperial administration. As they studied and wrote, they tended to forget the American scene, devoting more and more attention to the details of statesmanship and placemanship, commissions and bureaucracy in London. They were not unaware of their self-imposed limitations. Charles M. Andrews, in the preface to the fourth volume of *The Colonial Period of American History* (1934–1937), defined anew the boundaries of his concern: "Whether the colonial and commercial policies of the seventeenth and eighteenth century statesmen and capitalists were politically or economically sound or unsound is not the question; nor is it necessary at this point to determine the effects of these policies upon the colonists themselves or to compare them with present-day ideas. All I am attempting to do . . . is to make clear as best I may the essential features of these policies as England shaped them and to trace their history from the beginning of England's experience with colonies down to the eve of the American Revolution." And, a little later on, ". . . the subject forms an integral part of that most fundamental of colonial questions, the relationship which existed for more than one hundred and fifty years between England and her colonies overseas."

Of course, no two scholars of this "imperial" group followed exactly the same definition. Yet common to all was their conviction that the fundamental question as stated by Andrews —"the relationship . . . between England and her colonies overseas"—was exactly the right question. To answer it historians needed to know precisely what the Empire looked like, especially from its center in London. This emphasis left less and less energy to direct toward studies of the response of the colonists in America to imperial policies or to the indigenous development of social, economic, political—or any other— patterns within the colonies themselves. Despite this drift away from native shores, these scholars contributed a magnificent historical literature. They taught an understanding of the structure and the problems of Empire, breaking the older mold of colonial history which had seen significance only in terms of the American scene, substituting in its place a fuller, more realistic accounting of the colonies *as colonies* within a far-flung Empire. And, to a large extent, they liked what they saw. Viewing the Empire from London led them to sympathetic understanding of Britain's imperial problems and general satisfaction with the policies and agencies Britain devised to answer those problems.

But the age of the "imperialists" seemed to pass. Enchantment with their viewpoint and emphasis declined from its ready acceptance in the early decades of the twentieth century. There are many reasons why American colonial history, cast in the framework of British imperial history, should have become less satisfying than it was in the first half of the century. For the American of 1900 there might be exhilaration in the very idea of "empire" when empires, including a new American empire, were current political issues. To the citizen of the United States in 1917, a sympathetic study of British imperial problems in the eighteenth century might appear illuminating as he searched for Anglo-American understanding in a war-torn world. But increasingly, as economic and social and intellectual history turned aside older emphases on political and constitutional problems, historians began to desert the "imperial" stance and to return in their studies to the American scene.

Part of the reaction can be traced directly to the increasing emphasis on economic forces as determinants in human activities. The quarter-century from 1920 to 1945 saw the publication of studies which concentrated on economic motivations and economic effects instead of the institutions and policies Andrews had marked off as his field of interest. Andrews might be uninterested in the "soundness" of Britain's commercial policies or in their effect on the colonies, but Louis Hacker, Curtis Nettels, and a new generation were not. Hacker's studies encompassed the question of imperial relations largely as a part of his general writing on American capitalism, but his interpretation of the colonies' role in the British Empire emphasized the restrictive nature of the imperial connection. The questions Andrews put aside Hacker took up, and his answers to them described the economic effects of the Empire in dichotomous terms, with American merchant capitalism smothered by the mother country's restrictive policies, designed to favor British capitalists at the expense of the Americans. Curtis Nettels also sought to understand the effect of imperial regulation in terms of economic results and from them the attitudes of the people affected. The picture Nettels drew is not the portrait of collision between two aspiring capitalistic groups of Hacker's work; it is rather a mosaic of varied hues, with restrictions of serious consequences at some points, failures in policies at others, and colonial benefits at still others.

Hacker and Nettels were only two of many who found the "imperialist" version of history unsatisfactory. The disenchantment they represented was to be followed after 1945 by a further turn in interests and emphases. By then the cycle was almost complete. Thereafter the British Empire seemed no longer a satisfactory focus for investigation for many colonial historians. Increasingly in the years of the Cold War and its warmer moments, when the "American Way of Life" faced dire challenges, American scholars have searched for national origins within the local scene. They have recorded their findings in monographs of generally limited scope, often contenting themselves with biographies of colonial merchants, political leaders, molders of American thought. Or, if surveying instruments of political or economic regulation, they have centered their emphasis in the colonies, rather than in the imperial agencies.

Yet like all good history, the story of the American colonies in the British Empire continues to be a layered creation. No serious contemporary scholar ignores the findings, or cavalierly dismisses the interpretations, of the earlier "imperialists" or their present-day successors like Lawrence H. Gipson or Leonard W. Labaree. Although the emphasis has changed, the best colonial history still is written with an awareness of the problems of defining the place of the colonies in the Empire and with a curiosity to understand and attempt to assess the consequences of the imperial relationship for the Americans who lived in the seventeenth and eighteenth centuries.

One of the most obvious differences separating the "imperialists" and the newer "nationalists" (if they can be so termed) rises out of the separate ways in which the two groups viewed the nature of the British Empire. The "imperialists" generally assumed or believed that the imperial machinery

Britain created to supervise the Empire worked quite well. Britain and her colonies both benefited from the imperial relationship; imperial theories and the Empire in practice were basically one and the same. The more recent studies of American colonial origins, with their interest focused more closely upon the colonial scene, have emphasized evidence which suggests the opposite. The newer scholars have been impressed with the significance of the departure of the American colonists from the theoretical Empire, developing local controls and procedures which shifted actual power from the parent state to the colonies. In this view there were two empires: the Empire of theory and the Empire of reality. The first, and the one which the "imperialists" emphasized, was a relatively static enterprise. The other, the actual Empire, was constantly subjected to stresses and strains, and, as conceived by the American colonists at the close of the colonial era, was a very different entity than the theoretical Empire.

This difference in viewpoint between older and newer scholars is by no means the only problem of interpretation faced by students of America's early years. The pages which follow will indicate some of the other areas of disagreement among the expert craftsmen of history. However, before an analysis of the American colonies in the British Empire, either in theory or practice, can be undertaken, it is necessary to recount in brief fashion the story of the way in which that Empire was created. That task will occupy our attention for the remainder of this chapter.

MOTIVATIONS AND ASSUMPTIONS

The English people who were responsible for the creation of the first British Empire were motivated by three basic considerations. Englishmen built an Empire in the New World and exerted themselves to maintain that Empire for economic, strategic, and social reasons. These are broad classifications. Within any of them may be found a remarkable variety of expressions of interest and intent. Yet they are reasonably satisfactory labels for discussing the motivations for creation of the first British Empire.

Economically, England turned to her American possessions as an increasingly important element in building and maintaining her national strength. This attention to Empire may be seen in both the private and the public economic sectors in England. As trade with America increased during the seventeenth century, private entrepreneurs correspondingly concerned themselves with expanding their sources of profit, looking to the English state for such help as could be given. At the same time, the colonies provided royal revenues of considerable significance to the ruling Stuart kings and enhanced the national goal of building an independent, self-sufficient state. Within these broad objectives, private and public interests coincided and found expression in the relatively ill-defined, but nonetheless persuasive theories known as "mercantilism."

Both private economic interests and state planners believed that colonies would be useful to the mother country as sources of raw materials, producers of noncompetitive and, hopefully, strategic goods unavailable in the homeland, and as markets for fabricated products. The overseas dominions were to be perpetual dependencies which would and should always contribute to the accumulation of wealth in the parent state that would ensure the rising power of the English nation in the new age of costly warfare.

This economic impulse was the first major cause for the creation of the Empire; it remained a guiding motivation through the history of that first Empire. But, in time, other arguments attracted adherents and brought additional emphasis to Empire building. Toward the close of the seventeenth century, England entered the long series of wars with France which would lead ultimately to the impressive British triumphs in the Great War for Empire, ending in 1763. During this three-quarters of a century of Anglo-French rivalry, the American provinces of both contestants became increasingly significant in strategic planning. Englishmen who had long thought of the American outposts merely as economic dependencies accommodated their views to consider the colonies as strategic entities, vulnerable to attack by enemy forces but also useful as bases for operations against those same foes. Thus theoretical strategic advantages of American colonies, set forth much earlier by men like Richard Hakluyt, who had identified the potential benefit of colonies in opening opportunities by which England could strike against her then enemy, Spain, became realities in the eighteenth century.

In addition to economic impulses and strategic considerations, the outposts of Empire in the New World were also useful instruments for effecting social change. The colonies could be, and were, havens for oppressed people and conveniently distant dumping grounds for misfits and dissidents —the religiously unorthodox, the economically unemployed, the criminally convicted—all the potentially dangerous segments of the English population. The colonies could be, and were, useful as laboratories for social, sometimes even utopian, experimentation. The colonies could have been, but never fully became, the scene of religious endeavors, especially the conversion of the heathen to Protestant Christianity, or such intellectual pursuits as observing and recording the natural history of the untouched wilderness.

No carefully charted blueprint ever was drawn and adhered to, neatly balancing these various objectives. England never created a "yardstick" for precisely measuring imperial affairs against a set of established standards. In fact, imperial theories sometimes collided with each other, making choices among alternative actions difficult to determine. Equal emphasis never was placed on all objectives of the Empire at any one time or by all groups of people. Since the first British Empire lasted more than one hundred years, shifts in objectives and policies were to be expected. But a few relatively constant assumptions were held and remained basic in imperial thought throughout the era.

First was the assumption, altered in only a very few minor instances late in the era, that colony building was to be a private endeavor. The Crown was willing to donate, on its own terms, the real estate involved, and from time to time to grant some concessions to encourage the initial development of colonies. For example, in some cases trade concessions were provided for a limited number of years. But except for that, private resources were to be employed. It was up to the adventurers and businessmen of the time to accumulate the courage and the money to plant the outposts across the water. No royal funds could be called into action to promote the great goal of colony building.

Second, once established, the colonies were to remain perpetually in an inferior or subsidiary position to the parent state. For purposes of convenience in administration or for encouragement of particular purposes, the colonists might be allowed measures of limited local control, but, although unevenly applied, the basic assumption universally held in England was that the provinces were not, and as far as the future was concerned, never would be, equals with the mother country. There was no provision for eventually adopting mature colonies into organic union with the parent state. England would remain the center; the colonies would remain dependencies.

Finally, a third assumption was developed concerning diplomacy and defense. While local protection, mostly against hostile Indians, remained a colonial concern, as the collisions between England and France spread into the empires it became understood that England owed some obligation for providing security to her "wards" across the water. Varying greatly from time to time and place to place, by the end of the era the colonists and Britain both assumed that the major burden of defense would fall on the mother country, although some elements of a "partnership in war" were always expected and the colonists themselves were called upon to provide some contribution to the planning, leadership, manpower, and financing of imperial defense and expansion. Similarly, although "neighborhood agreements" were sometimes arranged, as, for example, between New England and New Netherlands, in establishing a temporary dividing line, diplomacy, like defense, was a matter for imperial rather than colonial determination.

While these assumptions—private rather than public investment in colonial enterprises, perpetual dependency, and imperial control of diplomacy and, eventually, defense—remained more or less permanent bases of imperial thought and action, the motivations for building and maintaining the Empire—economic, strategic, social—were constantly subjected to the environment and situation in the New World. Empires are not, by their very nature, unilateral operations. No matter how cleverly conceived an English policy might be in terms of furthering national interests at home, the fact always remained that the realities of the situation in America might make alterations necessary, or even bring defeat to the policy. So long as the statesmen engaged in formulating imperial policies provided room in their plans for adjustments to the realities of colonial life, their policies stood good chance of success. But often, given the distances involved, the slowness of communication, the natural tendencies for Englishmen to think in terms of the homeland and American colonists to think in terms of their own welfare, American realities modified and at times completely frustrated the "best laid plans" of England. How far American realities had moved from English theories was not completely apparent until after 1763, and then it was obvious that the same ideas of empire no longer satisfied parent and child. However, until that time, the assumptions seemed reasonably workable, and for the better part of the century, with adjustments and modifications smoothing out the rougher edges, the relationships between homeland and colonies continued to provide a framework within which both colonies and mother country experienced increasing prosperity, making Britain and her Empire the growing envy of much of Western Europe.

THE EARLY PLANTINGS

It is often asserted that England established her first Empire in a fit of absent-mindedness. Or, put another way, in the middle years of the seventeenth century, England seemed to "discover" the colonies which her people earlier had planted in the New World and began to consider those colonies in a changed way. Formerly, if thought of at all, they were viewed as isolated, individual outposts on the edge of the vast new continent of North America, variously conceived and maintained, but in no sense forming even a minor economic, and certainly not a strategic, unit of national strength. Then, in the days of the English Civil War and the years of the Restoration era that followed, those formerly almost forgotten outposts emerged into focus as properties potentially valuable to the realm, capable of being nurtured into economic assets and worthy of consideration as future sources of national strength.

Considering the fact that in the years between Jamestown's planting in 1607 and the beginnings of the English Civil War in 1641 more than 70,000 Englishmen had left their homeland for various parts of America, it is obvious that most Englishmen knew something about the colonies in the New World. Too much endeavor had been expended, too many pounds sterling of capital had been risked, too many lottery tickets had been purchased and missionary funds donated for there to have been no knowledge of the overseas activities. But what was true, and remained so throughout most of the history of the first British Empire, was that affairs at home and within the more familiar world of neighboring continental Europe crowded the mind. This priority of domestic and European concern was to continue throughout the seventeenth and eighteenth centuries. Under the circumstances, only a very few men were immediately and directly involved in overseas colonization. For that reason, and perhaps also because of the great variety of circumstances out of which the colonies had come into existence, decades passed before many Englishmen began to perceive over-all patterns in, and possibilities of common benefits from, the ill-assorted outposts in America.

By the time such considerations became important enough to be acted upon, and an Empire created, there existed in America a strange miscellany of adolescent colonies. These were grouped geographically in three regions: the Chesapeake area, where Virginians, the first of the colonists, and settlers in Maryland, the fief of the Calverts, were engaged in developing their tobacco society; the New England area, with

Massachusetts Bay as the hub, and the satellites of Plymouth, New Haven, Connecticut, Rhode Island, along with outposts in New Hampshire and Maine, clustered around; and, finally, in the Caribbean, the island possessions including St. Christopher, Antigua, Nevis, Montserrat, Barbados, and Bermuda.

Some of these colonies came into being as the offspring of trading companies chartered by the Crown, and some still retained that relationship. The constitutional theory undergirding such colonies was relatively uncomplicated. Possession of overseas lands claimed by England (fundamentally on John Cabot's official exploratory voyage of 1497) were the Crown's to dispose of as it saw fit. Venturesome merchants, anticipating profits from commerce, petitioned for royal permission to form chartered companies to engage in trade, exploration, and colonization. The technique had been used for a half-century to organize commercial enterprises in other parts of the world before it was applied in the trading company charter granted in 1606 by James I to the Virginia Company. The trading company charter also was used for the Massachusetts experiment in 1629. In that case, the charter was still intact. As for Virginia, by 1650 the company had been dissolved for a quarter of a century, and its offspring, the Virginia colony, had come under direct royal control. It might be noted, however, that the institution of royal control paradoxically allowed more opportunities for local direction of affairs than company ownership had permitted.

A second type of royal grant had resulted in a differently structured group of colonies. The Crown had seen fit to bestow upon individuals or groups of individuals proprietary privileges to certain parts of the American continent. The Caribbean islands, Maryland, and, by sub-grants, certain parts of New England, had been disposed of in this way and still were connected legally to the homeland (that is, to the Crown) through the thread of these proprietary patents.

Finally, there were indigenously created covenant-type settlements, which legally and constitutionally rested on no royal sanction at all, but rather were the result of settlers taking matters of government and the internal organization of their communities into their own hands, forming their own political structures. Connecticut and the Rhode Island communities had come into being in this fashion.

Thus England's American outposts, as of 1650, shared no single type of legal tie with the mother country. In the untidy mixture could be found four distinct styles of colonial structures: royal province, trading company endeavors, proprietary colonies, and covenant communities. In time this bureaucratic nightmare, lacking all semblance of uniformity, would engage the talents and imaginations of men dedicated to the task of reducing the colonies to a common pattern.

The untidiness of the constitutional relationships between the American colonies and England was matched, or surpassed, by the variety of impulses responsible for the creation and initial settlement of the outposts. In no case was the settlement of any colony the result of a single, exclusive motive. While hope for economic gain might appear the most significant force motivating the members of the Virginia Company, a variety of other impulses also generated some of their hopes and aspirations —religiously inspired dreams of converting the heathen natives; patriotic purpose in crowding close to and contesting with Spain her New World empire; adventuresomeness which needed outlet and found it in the strange new lands across the western seas. In the same way, to picture early Massachusetts Bay as an exclusively religious enterprise, and fail to consider the social and economic aspirations of its founders, creates a distorted portrait.

And if common patterns did not exist for the constitutional relationships between these individual enterprises in America and the homeland, or in the mixtures and balances of motivations that had brought them into being, the same is true, and even amplified, in the colonies' development after their initial settlement. Many elements and ingredients combined to produce such varied results. Geography, climate, intent of sponsors, the natural resources of the land, the types of colonists attracted to the settlement—these and many other variables were responsible for the mosaic design. Yet even here some classification is possible. In New England, self-sustaining agriculture, with other emphases upon fish and timber for export, along with increasing interest in general commercial activities, became the pattern of life. The Chesapeake area, after false starts in such directions as gold seeking and silk culture, had, by mid-century, already adopted a tobacco economy, although it then lacked the elements of huge plantations and the predominantly Negro slave labor force which would characterize it later. The Caribbean islands turned as naturally to the sugar products they could grow so profitably and which, in English eyes, were blessed because they did not compete with home production.

Thus neither in constitutional structure, nor founders' purposes, nor economic development did England's American settlements share common patterns. Generally isolated from each other by huge stretches of forests, during the first three decades of successful English settlement the colonies amounted to little more than struggling beach-heads, precariously poised on the edge of the American coastline. Of course these New World Englishmen did not have the continent all to themselves. They shared it with the natives, and with Europeans from Spain and France, Holland, and Sweden. The Spanish were the most feared and the most envied, for they seemed to have found the richest parts of the New World and had grown powerful from the fortunes they had shipped back to Europe. Yet even at this time, English fears were evaporating. The fact that island properties in the West Indies, so close to New Spain, could be colonized was impressive in itself, and soon new plans were afoot to contest even further the Spanish hold on the Caribbean. The French, like the English, were only beginning to reap success from their colonizing ventures, centered in the St. Lawrence Valley. Contacts between Englishmen and Frenchmen in the New World in the first half of the century primarily were limited to the fishing areas off the Newfoundland shores. The Dutch, who soon had reduced the Swedish enterprises on the Delaware River, were somewhat more obviously in the way, for their holdings in the area of future New York not only geographically separated the New England and Chesapeake settlements, but also offered the Dutch merchants a base of operations from which to trade within the English colonies.

In time direct contests with these neighboring European colonizers would take place, but for the immediate moment there were other events to consider. In fact, as of 1641 a curtain descended even on new planting activities in English America. For the next two decades, the homeland was torn internally by civil war, the demolition of royal rule, the execution of Charles I, the institution of Parliamentary rule, the Protectorate of Oliver Cromwell, and finally the return to the monarchy, with the restoration of Charles II. In such times there could be little inclination and less energy for new colonizing activities in America.

STEPS TOWARD EMPIRE

Despite the lull in initiating new colonial ventures, however, the twenty years from 1640 to 1660, in many ways, were as significant an era for the future British Empire in America as any other twenty-year period until the time of the American Revolution, more than a century later. The contest in England between Crown and Parliamentary forces, culminating in the demise of royal rule, brought two major considerations concerning America to the attention of policy makers. First, the elimination of royal control brought into question the constitutional bases upon which the American colonies were founded. At about the same time, commercial rivalries with other European nations caused some Englishmen to look upon the nation's overseas outposts as something more than separate, isolated communities and to view the American colonies in a different perspective, as units of a potentially integrated, expanded "Empire" beyond the seas.

The first of these new considerations arose from the developments within revolutionary England itself. When Parliament replaced the Crown as the supreme power in England, what, if any, alterations were required in the constitutional relationships with the overseas colonies? Those colonies, so far as they were bound to England, were bound to the Crown: Virginia under direct royal control; Massachusetts, Maryland, and the West Indian possessions by royal charters. As Parliament assumed authority at home, Crown rights and powers became Parliament's, and that seemed to include control of the American dominions. But events in some parts of the New World soon demonstrated that some of the colonists thought differently.

The New England settlements, it was believed, would cause no great amount of trouble. Puritan themselves, they were expected to look with favor upon events in England. Ironically, it is true, the leading New England community, Massachusetts Bay, used the occasion of Parliament's step to supremacy at home to develop for itself an even more boldly conceived posture as an independent republican community, developing even more highly its uniquely separate and independent theories of localism. The Chesapeake and West Indian provinces, however, were a different matter. In Virginia both the legislature and the royal governor, William Berkeley, had denied the legitimacy of the revolutionary English government, insisting on continuing their allegiance and devotion to the deposed Stuart family. In Maryland, where the proprietor's fellow Catholics had been struggling against Puritan settlers for some time, a similar declaration of allegiance to the Stuart cause issued from the proprietor's governor.

Retraction of such statements of disobedience to the new regime was required, and in 1650 Parliament enacted a coercive statute, dispelling all questions or doubts about its intention to establish supremacy over the colonies. The act set forth a licensing system for all foreign vessels trading to America and a temporary commercial prohibition against the wayward provinces of Maryland, Virginia, and those Caribbean islands which had also proclaimed loyalty to Charles. In time a Parliamentary commission arrived in the New World to receive the submission of the provinces to the Commonwealth government. Once reduced to acknowledgment of Parliamentary supremacy, the colonies were constitutionally "established" in fashion acceptable to the English authorities.

More significant (in terms of later development of the Empire) than this tidying up of constitutional relationships between parent state and colonial children was the new way the Puritan regime in England viewed the American colonies as part of a larger, total unit—as something like a young empire. Reflections of this different concept of overseas enterprises are apparent in the "Western Design" of Oliver Cromwell, an ambitious blueprint for direct contest with Spain in the New World. Before the Cromwellian era had run its course, the "Design" would bring conquest of Jamaica and inclusion of that island into the orbit of English control.

And even more portentous as a reflection of "imperial" thought was the Parliamentary enactment of the first comprehensive commercial legislation regarding the New World colonies. The Navigation Act of 1651 implemented the principles of the coercive legislation of the previous year and carried even further the commercial regulation laid down by that statute. Designed to bring ultimate superiority to England's mercantile operations within the English "Empire," the Act of 1651 set forth a basic prohibition closing the trade of the colonies to all except shippers from England or other English colonies.

This was neither the first commercial regulation regarding the colonies, nor was it the first time that Parliament, as an agency, had legislated regarding overseas possessions. Earlier the tobacco trade had been regulated, and imports into England from the Chesapeake plantations had been given a favored position in the kingdom, including a prohibition against tobacco culture within the realm. At the same time, tobacco from America had been subjected to importation duties of some significance to the royal treasury, suffering constant, chronic depletion. Also Parliament, at earlier times, legislated against foreign trade with the American dominions, but that legislation had gone largely ignored and unenforced.

The new statute in 1651, however, because of its comprehensive nature and its objectives, signaled the beginnings of a long series of Parliamentary measures, stretching in time forward for the next one hundred years, each enactment more closely defining the commercial and industrial roles allowed to the American colonies. Thus the act stands as one of the more significant milestones along the road leading to the creation of an empire. And the act, itself largely economic in motivation, gives indication that, at the beginning, the creation of an empire was very much an economic consideration.

Because it does stand as the first comprehensive statement of England's economic policy toward her American dominions, this Parliamentary measure of 1651 has been of more than ordinary interest to historians searching for the origins of the first British Empire. There has been some disagreement among the experts regarding the specific conditions of 1651 resulting in the enactment of the general policies. It seems clear from what has been written about the antecedents to the act that it marked no sudden departure from previous attempts at commercial regulation, attempts extending backward in time through some centuries as far as over-all English trade was concerned, and through some decades as far as such measures touched colonial commerce. And it also indicates the generally accepted English mercantilist view of national interest, which was by no means a startling innovation in English thought as of 1651.

Even so, granting the antecedents and earlier general acceptance of the basic purposes of the act, Charles M. Andrews' views (which have been subjected to considerable analysis and, in some cases, rejection by historians) appear to retain validity. In *The Colonial Period of American History,* Andrews asserted that the immediate cause of the Parliamentary enactment of 1651 was the growing success of Dutch merchants in carrying away the exports from England's Caribbean and Chesapeake possessions. Commercial rivalry with the Dutch, if it was eventually to end in British superiority, needed to be defined in such a way that England's own colonies did not contribute to Dutch strength. Since the Dutch had been particularly successful in their competition with the English in the American trade, the exclusion of all foreigners from the dominions, if properly enforced, would rid the English merchants trading to America of that competition, build England's mercantile strength generally, and in so doing advance the over-all national strength as well.

Thus, by 1660, England had experienced the initial stirrings toward Empire. The supreme authority from "home" had quieted restless disloyalty to its regime; a flurry of interest had been generated looking toward an expansion of overseas activities; and, most significant of all, the rudiments of a system of commercial regulation had been legislated. Out of the turmoil of revolutionary England had come the first tokens of a new entity—an English Empire in the New World.

THE RESTORATION EMPIRE

In 1660 the Puritan government fell and the Stuart family was restored to the English throne. While the next three decades would see the emergence of relatively consistent efforts to construct an orderly, logically arranged empire in the New World, the motivation leading to such efforts was not completely new. What had been begun during the Interregnum would be continued and expanded, for the regulation of overseas commerce for the benefit of the homeland proved as pleasant and desirable to the forces ruling post-Restoration England as it had been to the merchant groups sponsoring the policies during the period of Parliamentary supremacy. Charles II's return to England brought involvement from a greater variety of interest groups, but it was not a question of competition over alternative policies, for imperial regulation held promise of benefits for all of the groups.

Not only was there continued desire on the part of English merchants for protection against Dutch and other foreign competitors in the American trade; increasingly other specialized economic interests in England would look for extension of regulatory enactments to protect or expand their particular interests. Charles himself was vitally concerned with such regulation, for the obvious reason that the Crown would gain revenues from effective imperial control of colonial commerce. And, as regulation was extended and the need to administer more effectively the policies laid down was realized, there grew up in the department and commission offices in England a group of imperially minded servants of the state, a more or less permanent group of men, some high-ranking lords, other civil service placemen, committed to the concept of building a British Empire. To further the welfare and interests of the state, these men perceived it their duty to more precisely define and regulate the overseas colonies, and generally they believed this could be most easily effected by furthering unity among and control over the American dominions.

As the Empire builders turned to their tasks in the quarter-century following the Restoration, they had more component parts available for structuring an Empire than had been in existence in 1660. In relatively rapid order the already established settlements in America were joined by new planting endeavors. By the early 1680's four new colonial entities had been created. Between the Delaware River and the New England settlements, where the Dutch had operated commercial ventures from their American outpost, the English, after conquest of the Dutch settlements, shaped their acquisition into two proprietary enterprises—New York and New Jersey. Across the Delaware River, another proprietary province was begun by William Penn. And south of Virginia, in lands still claimed by Spain, Charles II carved out the proprietary grant called Carolina for a group of his friends and supporters.

While the forces motivating the expansion of England into the areas of New York and New Jersey, Pennsylvania and Carolina were mixed, and the development of those new provinces varied greatly, common to all was the use of the proprietary patent as the constitutional basis for settlement. The consistency in use of this form is indicative of the dominant political forces in Restoration England. No longer were trade and commerce the prime motives leading to overseas colonization; merchants and capitalists, by 1660, had come to understand that profits from initiating colonies could not be counted on while, conversely, the rewards from trade with already established colonies were of considerable potential. Nor was religious refuge any longer a major objective for most such new colonial endeavors, although Pennsylvania provides an exception and in no case can the religious impulse be entirely discounted.

The basic impulse leading to these new proprietaries was

the interest of the landed aristocratic class in England—men who, in the light of their own experience as landholders in England, looked upon English America primarily as a place to extend their land-holding and their income. The use of the proprietary charter to gain the opportunity for such increase in landed wealth, although utilizing a more antique form than the joint stock company charter, symbolizes the dominance of the landed English group in the formation of these new enterprises.

The form is not paradoxical in relationship to the dominant group supporting the Restoration government at home, but it is ironic that, at the same time Charles I severed large stretches of his American real estate from Crown control, handing over those areas to others as perpetual proprietaries, other men in the kingdom, including close advisers to the king, were beginning to visualize the American colonies in more imperialistic terms which, if such plans were ever to succeed, demanded greater consolidation and control. Charles encouraged both groups at the same time, with one hand separating areas of North America from immediate royal control and with the other hand encouraging a policy of administering the dominions in a more efficient and, hopefully, more economically rewarding way.

It should be pointed out, however, that while the Carolina and Duke of York grants of the 1660's tended, like the earlier Calvert patent, to place sweeping personal powers in the hands of the proprietors, by 1681 when the Pennsylvania grant was made to William Penn, the forces urging consolidation were able to exert rather significant restrictions upon that proprietor's powers. Among other clauses of Penn's charter reducing his authority and bringing Pennsylvania under closer royal control were the stipulations that laws of the province must be referred to the Privy Council for approval or disallowance; that the right of appeal to English courts must be open to settlers in the province; that an agent must be maintained in England to answer any charges of evasion of the navigation laws or other complaints; and that the local administration must co-operate with the customs officials established in the colony. These limitations on the proprietor's authority all are indicative of the changes that had come in imperial thought in the two decades since the Restoration.

The task of bringing orderly arrangements in relationships between the older, existing colonies and the parent state was also an objective of the post-Restoration policy makers. The work to be done naturally varied from colony to colony because of the variety of previous arrangements that had been forged. In Virginia the task was relatively simple: restoration of Crown rule was implemented in this oldest of the American dominions without difficulty merely by returning the constitutional relationship to what it had been before the demise of royal control in England, even to the re-establishment of Sir William Berkeley to his former governorship. In the other Chesapeake colony, despite desires on the part of some of the imperial planners to see Calvert's control extinguished, the province of Maryland (which had been restored to the proprietor in 1658) was continued in his control.

The pattern of reconstituting royal control in the West Indian areas was also rather clearly defined. Barbados, the Leeward Islands (St. Christopher, Nevis, Antigua, and Montserrat), and, at an even earlier date, the newly captured Spanish island of Jamaica were constituted royal provinces. In Barbados and the Leewards this meant reduction of a former proprietary; in Jamaica it meant transference from military rule to civilian control in royal form.

New England offered other situations. Rhode Island was desirous of exchanging the Parliamentary-based charter that Roger Williams had secured in 1644 for a royal acknowledgment of the colony's existence; Connecticut sought the same security. Both colonies were fortunate, for despite later attempts by Charles II and his successor to reduce colonies to Crown control, in the first years of his rule Charles agreed to grant royal charters for the two colonies, liberally accepting the places as corporate entities and allowing them to continue with their basically democratic governments. Thus Rhode Island, which had fought desperately to retain its identity against encroachments by its "orthodox" Puritan neighbors, and Connecticut, now also encompassing the New Haven colony within its borders, reached an early and, for themselves, very satisfactory solution to their problem of legitimatizing their independent status as nearly self-governing corporations.

Massachusetts Bay proved a different story. Her defiant attitude expressed during the Puritan regime in England, reflecting what Michael G. Hall (in *The Glorious Revolution in America,* 1964) has called the province's *"de facto* independence," could hardly be expected to abate with the return to power of the old enemy, the Stuart monarchy. Prosperous, powerful, and determined to retain local control of her destiny, the Bay Province was marked for special consideration by the post-Restoration Empire builders. The "battle," however, proved a lengthy affair, and before its conclusion was reached, England had moved a long way toward its goal of a consolidated Empire in the New World.

During the first decade and a half following the Restoration, England not only continued but expanded and extended the mercantile regulations begun by the Navigation Act of 1651 and, in addition, created both in the colonies and at home more efficient methods for administering the commercial laws. Since the Parliamentary Act of 1651 was of doubtful legality once Charles had been restored as king of England, some reenactment of the legislation was to be expected. Also to be considered was the fact that none of the American provinces had voluntarily complied with the act and in most of the colonies outright hostility to the regulations had been expressed. But rather than a mere restatement of that act, new legislation in 1660 (often termed the First Navigation Act) extended economic regulation to include a specific provision that in the case of certain significant staple products grown in the colonies, such as sugar, tobacco, and cotton, exportation from the place of production was allowed only to England or to another English colony. Thus was begun the practice of listing or "enumerating" certain strategic commodities for shipment only within the Empire or, if surpluses were not needed there, at least to be cleared from English ports in transshipment to other parts of the world, thereby insuring the carriage profits to English merchants and revenue proceeds to the Crown.

Next was added, in legislation of 1663 (the Staple Act), a formula for protecting the English merchant community interested in the American trade. This provision required that European goods destined for importation into the American colonies must be shipped via the homeland. A few commodities, including salt to New England, wine from the Azores and Madeira, and horses and servants from Ireland, were excepted. All else was subject to handling by English merchants, insuring them a monopoly in the source of manufactured goods brought to the colonies.

Ten years later a further Parliamentary enactment closed a loophole left in the process of regulating enumerated goods. Merchants had presumably satisfied the earlier requirements by simply stopping at a colonial port after loading enumerated goods and then trading those goods outside the Empire. Now export duties, roughly equivalent to the English importation duties, were required on enumerated products at the time they left the colonial port of origin. This enactment was particularly significant for future relationships between England and her American colonies, since the duties required something more than haphazard enforcement by colonial governors. The need to provide orderly and efficient duty collections introduced customs officials into America. For the first time there now appeared in the English colonies a group of imperial office-holders specifically charged with enforcement of the trade laws.

While administrative posts were thus established in America, there was also created, in 1675, a new agency in England responsible for overseeing the imperial trade. After a variety of short-lived and generally less than satisfactory experiments with committees and commissions, the agency known as the Lords of Trade was created, charged with overall supervision of colonial affairs. A committee of Privy Councilors, the Lords of Trade, developed its own administrative staff, through whose offices information about the colonies could be funneled and colonial affairs could be "cleared." Through its own appointed agents sent to America, the Lords of Trade could gather additional knowledge of colonial events upon which new policies for bringing order into imperial affairs could be built.

Thus, within the first fifteen years following the Restoration of Stuart rule, an expanded mercantile regulatory system, involving more centralized agencies than had been known before in England and entirely new officers on the American side of the Atlantic, had been established. While the plans were yet incomplete, and further movements in the direction of consolidation of the Empire would be made later, by the mid-1670's, Empire building had progressed a considerable distance.

REACTION IN AMERICA

The introduction of the new customs officers into the American colonies, necessitated by the Navigation Act of 1673, brought colonial theories and imperial regulations into a new focus for Americans. Flesh-and-blood men were now physically present in the colonies, charged with making the Empire work as a day-to-day affair. Tied to these activities in America was the new agency, the Lords of Trade in England, directing colonial affairs in a more centralized fashion than had ever been attempted before.

This was not only a matter of enforcing laws which perhaps had not been obeyed; this involved positions to be filled by men with a variety of motivations for their actions; it introduced both a cluster of individuals in positions of power in England espousing doctrines and concepts about the proper relationships between colonies and parent state and, even more potentially explosive, the arrival in America of Englishmen in a capacity never known before—agents of the new Empire, interested in the colonies as sources of national strength *and* personal fortune, but often, unfortunately, unaware of the local, colonial circumstances affecting the Americans' attitudes toward the new regulations.

At one time historians were relatively content to trace

the origins and development of the structure of regulation; to delineate the statutes of Parliament and the actions of the Lords of Trade and other English agencies that brought the rudiments of an empire into existence. But increasingly of late, a further dimension has been added to our knowledge of the first British Empire—detailed analyses of the personalities involved in administering those regulations, which show, in addition to what the structure of empire was, the way in which it was actually put into operation. Michael G. Hall's study, *Edward Randolph and the American Colonies* (1960), is especially useful in this way, for the author analyzes both Randolph's motivations and the colonists' reactions to him and to his policies. Randolph was not only an advance agent of Empire, making his way along the Atlantic coast of the American colonies as the authorized eyes and ears of the Lords of Trade; he was an ambitious office seeker and fortune hunter, who looked upon the national interests of England and his own personal advancement as complementary, rather than competitive, objectives. He was, writes Bernard Bailyn in *The New England Merchants in the Seventeenth Century* (1955), ". . . characteristic of a whole class of Englishmen now beginning to arrive in the colonies. These men—customs functionaries, lesser bureaucrats, fortune hunters in official positions—found careers for themselves in the quickly expanding colonial administration."

Randolph's career in the American colonies was particularly focused on the New England region, and especially on Massachusetts Bay. That Puritan colony was to experience a series of threatening gestures by the new imperialists, for upon the goal of bringing ordered relationships between the parent state and the Bay Province hinged much of the imperialists' hopes for the consolidation and unification of all of the American colonies. This unique attention to Massachusetts was prompted partly by the fact that the Bay Colony was the hub of the northern possessions, generally prosperous, growing in population, and determinedly maintaining a posture of independent action that mocked at the new regulations and threatened failure for the imperialists.

In matters of commerce, the Massachusetts people had demonstrated an unwillingness to comply with Parliament's first attempts at trade regulation during Cromwell's years. And there was more to the Bay Province's attitude than merely the desire to continue profitable trading outside the imperial regulations. The Bay people had questioned the authority of Parliament to legislate concerning their trade, and presumably any other matter, resting their interpretation of their constitutional guarantees on the terms of their 1629 charter from Charles I.

Thus, among the early actions of the restored monarch, in 1664 Charles II had dispatched to New England a commission to receive the "surrender" to his authority of the people there. The terms requested were not particularly severe, but the Massachusetts authorities continued their defiant attitude and no "surrender" was forthcoming. Neighboring Rhode Island and Connecticut, undoubtedly relieved to have settled their problems in the charters of the previous years, prudently complied with the commissioners' requests; Massachusetts moved not one inch. As a result, the reports from the commission were highly critical of the Bay Province, complaining of violations of the Acts of Trade, limited voting privileges to members of the Puritan congregations, competitive economic activities that threatened harm to England's own economy. Ordered to send representatives to England to answer the commission's charges, the Massachusetts authorities delayed action and for a full decade (while London burned in the Great Fire, England suffered the ravages of the plague and fought a war with the Dutch) escaped further attention.

But then, after ten years, the "breathing-spell" ran out, and by the mid-1670's the deferred issues had again been raised. In this new act of the drama, Edward Randolph played an integral role, for he had secured from the newly created Lords of Trade a commission as agent for inspecting the Massachusetts province. His reports sent back to the Trade Lords formed the basis for new actions against the province. The debate that ensued consumed eight years—years full of continued agitation both from Randolph and his allies in America and from the new imperialists in England, looking toward a cancellation of the Massachusetts charter and a reconstruction of the colony, probably as a royal province. These were years full of spirited defense by the Massachusetts authorities as they attempted to counter the threats and thrusts against them.

The battle, for Massachusetts, was a losing game; decision after decision went against her. The colony's claims to New Hampshire were denied and by 1679 the establishment of a royal government there ended all hopes that the place might be retained. Similarly, the Bay Colony's claims to Maine were ruled invalid and only by purchasing the rights awarded other claimants was it possible for Massachusetts to continue her control there. Finally the worst blow of all fell, the Lords of Trade initiating legal action in the Court of Chancery in England against the Massachusetts charter. That court ruled, in 1684, that the patent was forfeit, and independent Massachusetts was now at the mercy of the Crown, with no chartered rights at all.

After the reduction of the charter, it might have been expected that Massachusetts would be restructured as a royal province, like Virginia, but the course of events in England altered any such possibility. Charles II died in 1685 and was succeeded on the throne by his brother James II. As proprietor of New York, James had gained some definite ideas about the proper reconstruction of the northern parts of his American empire. During the first year of his rule, imperial reorganization and the drive toward consolidation of the American empire reached its highest level of experimentation. Rather than merely bringing Massachusetts under direct royal control, there was now instituted a comprehensive revision of the entire governing structure for the northern colonies in the instrument termed the Dominion of New England.

The Dominion was to include all of the New England colonies—New Hampshire, Massachusetts, Rhode Island, Plymouth, and Connecticut—as well as New York and New Jersey, and plans were pushed to eventually include Pennsylvania as well. Over this Dominion was to be placed a royally appointed governor, who would be aided in his administration by a lieutenant governor for the New York area and an appointed council. No provision was included for representative colonial assemblies. The elected legislative houses of the various component colonies were abolished, and direct control from England was to be instituted.

In terms of England's objectives, her theories of empire, and the desires of that group of imperialists dedicated to those theories and goals, the Dominion made sense. But the plan ignored the historical and current realities of the American colonies, and if it were ever to succeed it would require both enlightened administration and time. Neither of these elements proved to be present. Sir Edmund Andros, the governor of the Dominion, upon whom so much of its success or failure would depend, was lacking in the patience and the tact necessary to forward intelligently the aims of the reorganization. And time, which was perhaps the most essential of all ingredients, proved to be equally non-existent. Within three years James would flee from England, allowing in the moment termed the Glorious Revolution the re-establishment of the monarchy in a new form, under the new sovereigns, William III and his wife Mary. Those events in England would see their counterparts in the New World as the Glorious Revolution helped spawn a series of smaller revolutions in the American colonies, washing away the reorganized structure of imperial control as surely as the revolution in England had washed away the Catholic rule of James II.

A REBELLION IN VIRGINIA

The last quarter of the seventeenth century was the beginning of a testing time for the machinery of imperial control which had been fabricated during the years since mid-century. It was also a time of continuous refinement and extension of those imperial policies, leading to the attempted consolidation in the Dominion of New England. By the mid-1670's, Empire building had become a two-way street, with American reactions to English policies becoming an increasingly significant element in the workings of the imperial machinery. By the end of the century it was obvious that the first British Empire not only would be shaped by policy makers in the homeland, but would also be modified in form and function by the realities of American colonial life. The results, in many instances, were compromises.

Clarence Ver Steeg, in *The Formative Years, 1607–1763* (1964), has suggested a fruitful way of looking at the colonials' reactions to imperial policies during this era. He sees the American colonies as entering an era of "social instability"; he views these years as a time when a colonist's place in his community and society was not clearly charted and his actions reflected the uncertainty with which he confronted both present and future. These were the years of awkward adolescence for the colonies. The Americans had succeeded in sustaining themselves during the difficult, hazardous years of planting; they had taken on their local economic and social characteristics. But the early, founding generation was now gone. In its place were the sons and daughters of the founders (augmented, of course, by many newcomers) struggling to set patterns and control events in such a way that their particular objectives might be obtainable and that the early promise of the "good life," freed from the restrictions of the Old World, might be brought to fruition in the New World. In the early years, it had been expected that life in America would be patterned on the English model, but by 1680 there were colonists who had never known England. This fact, along with the necessary adjustments caused by the American environment, had created a situation in which older social structures were withering away and new social structures were in the process of creation.

This same freeing of men from previous concepts of well-ordered relationships, where "each man knew what was expected of him," Daniel Boorstin, in *The Americans: The Colonial Experience* (1958), has described as a major "promise" of New World life, imparting an essential ingredient to the "flavor" of America. It was what most sharply distinguished the colonial society from life in England. But the moments of recognition that the old was changing, the new arriving—in other words, exactly those last two decades of the seventeenth century when a generation of Americans searched for patterns not clearly discernible—are the years Ver Steeg describes as particularly characterized by social instability.

What happened in Empire building during those years was conditioned by events and situations both in England and America, and for America it was a time of uncertainty and trouble. Within the twenty years from 1675 to 1695, colonial life was beset with a variety of discordant episodes, including Indian wars, economic dislocations, the Salem witch hunt, and a series of rebellions—against a royal governor in Virginia, against proprietary rule in Maryland, against the newly instituted Dominion of New England in Massachusetts and New York. Historians studying the events of those years have become increasingly aware of the complexity of elements composing the recipes for trouble. In no one instance is it possible to relate a single-track story of English regulations opposed by militant American colonists who objected to those controls, revolted against them, and began, a century before its time, the "prologue" to the American Revolution. These were seventeenth-century crises, of a different sort from those that would come in the next century. But in the "unhinged" condition of American society, in the disorganized state of political groupings, in the disunified attitudes of colonists toward English policies are to be found some of the complex reasons for the local divisions which, becoming intermixed with personalities and policies of imperial change, created the variety of American responses to the new Empire.

In the events in Virginia of the years 1676–1677, it appears that the influence of the mother country's policies can be observed in only two of the many elements that were compounded to form Bacon's Rebellion. One of these was the basic constitutional fact that the appointed royal governor of the province, Sir William Berkeley, stood as the King's representative in Virginia, with his powers and authority derived from his royal commission and instructions. But to a large extent, this was not a determining factor among the forces shaping the rebellion, for, if involved at all, it appears to have been Berkeley's use of his authority, his personal decisions within that large area allowed to him to form policies, rather than his constitutional powers, that some of the rebelling colonists objected to. The revolt may have been anti-Berkeley, but it does not appear to have been anti-British.

The second feature of the episode that was directly related to the Empire was derived from the impact of the navigation laws upon the economy of Virginia. Tobacco had been enumerated, and thus could be exported only to ports within the Empire under the terms of the Navigation Act of 1660. It was also one of the American products most affected by the prohibition against colonial exportation in foreign vessels. As the Acts of Trade were administered, it became apparent that the profitable trade relations the Virginians had enjoyed with the Dutch carriers, especially during the years of the Interregnum, were a thing of the past. The Virginia tobacco economy declined, although how much that decline resulted from shipping shortages occasioned by the prohibition on foreign vessels, or from enumeration, or from overproduction within Virginia, is debatable. At any rate, only so far as economic depression was a cause of Bacon's Rebellion, and only to the extent that Virginians believed the restrictions of the trade acts responsible for the falling price of tobacco (and this they seem to have done), can the episode be viewed as an anti-imperial outbreak.

The causes of the uprising must be sought primarily within Virginia itself. The rebellion has been particularly studied in recent years by two historians who are far from agreement in their assessment of the events. Their disagreement rests upon their judgments of the two major protagonists in the troubles—the leader of the rebellion, Nathaniel Bacon, and the royal governor, Sir William Berkeley.

To Thomas Jefferson Wertenbaker, who has presented his interpretation in a variety of publications, including a book entitled *Torchbearer of the Revolution* (1940), Bacon is the hero of the era, a true forerunner of the Patriots of 1776 who championed, fought for, and finally died in the cause of American liberty endangered by English restrictions sponsored by tired old reactionary William Berkeley. In Wertenbaker's view, Bacon was a somewhat reluctant, but nonetheless true leader of the oppressed Virginia citizenry, a people downtrodden by a governor who ruled the province for fifteen years without elections, inept at Indian diplomacy and unable to defend the frontier settlements against raids by the tribesmen; a royal governor who misused his powers to reward his friends and himself, and who cared little for the rest of the Virginia population.

Bacon, the young hero, led his citizen band against this arbitrary system which Berkeley had fastened upon the Old Dominion, and finally died in the struggle. While nothing could save the leader from his untimely death, or those of his followers who were executed for their part in the uprising by Berkeley after he had regained power, vindication for the rebels was forthcoming with the arrival of a royal commission to investigate the affair, the recalling of Berkeley to England, and, especially, the events of a century later when other Virginians —Washington, Jefferson, Henry, the Lees—joined their fellow colonists in America to wage another rebellion in the name of and for the cause of freedom. "Let us not forget," writes Wertenbaker, "that though the sun of American liberty sank blood red across the James as the old governor sent one patriot after another to the gallows, it was the same sun which rose a century later to shine down upon the triumph of the man we call the Father of His Country."

Against this version of the events in Virginia, 1676–1677, consider the findings of another scholar, Wilcomb E. Washburn, whose study *The Governor and the Rebel* (1957) presents the same episode in quite a different light. Washburn emphasizes the Virginia frontiersmen's aggressiveness in Indian policy, the role of a popular Governor Berkeley in attempts to limit the acquisitive drive for land and Indian spoliation, the shifting social, economic, and political status of large and "ordinary" planters, as well as economic depression and the personality conflicts coloring the Bacon-Berkeley relationships. But in all this, says Washburn, Bacon was no liberal leader of a leveling movement, Berkeley no tyrant exercising despotic powers over a half-enslaved people. And, for our purposes here, the revolt, in this view, was certainly not an anti-English uprising, not in origins and especially not in results.

Even so, one final note might be appended. Wesley Frank Craven, in *The Southern Colonies in the Seventeenth Century* (1949), has suggested that "by no means the least significant feature of Bacon's Rebellion" was the speed with which the English government reacted to the news from Virginia and the dispatching, along with a special commission of investigation, of an expedition of eleven vessels and more than 1,100 soldiers under the command of Berkeley's successor, Colonel Herbert Jeffreys. Craven suggests that the arrival in Virginia of this force constituted an impressive symbol of the new imperial power, which must have been apparent to the colonists. Independence certainly was not an issue in Virginia at the time, yet the quickness of the royal response displays a sensitivity in imperial relationships indicative of the new Empire. "Thoughtful men must have recognized that these soldiers represented a purpose destined to have enduring influence on the life of the colony."

OTHER REBELLIONS

About the time that Bacon's uprising in Virginia was challenging the authority of Governor Berkeley, the New England communities found themselves involved in the most serious Indian uprising in their history. King Philip's War was to tax the financial and military resources of the New England colonies severely before the conflict had run its course. Yet, although distressingly disruptive, that was only one of the several calamities visiting the northern colonies at the time. Hard on its heels came the depressing news of Massachusetts' loss of New Hampshire, the adverse decision regarding the Bay Colony's claims to Maine, the loss of Massachusetts' charter, and, finally, the institution of the Dominion of New England.

As Bacon's Rebellion in Virginia had demonstrated social instability in that province, so the arrival of the Dominion Governor, Sir Edmund Andros, and his institution of the new order in Massachusetts Bay, exposed uncertainties and divisions within that colony's population. Bernard Bailyn, in his study of *The New England Merchants in the Seventeenth Century,* has shown that the events leading to the overthrow of Andros and his Dominion were far from simple black-and-white contests between liberty-loving Americans and a tyrannically arbitrary Dominion governor. Bailyn has demonstrated the divisions within Massachusetts and the dichotomy that had developed there between the older, inwardly oriented Puritan leadership, resisting change and determined to return as nearly as possible to the "Golden Age" of Massachusetts' independence (c. 1630–1660) on the one hand, and the interests and inclinations of newly rising men, many of them merchants, who could see the future welfare of the colony, and their own personal well-being, related to an extended role for Massachusetts within the framework of the English Empire.

Massachusetts as a closed society, apart from the mainstream of the western world, constantly purifying its society and building ever closer to the goal of God's Zion on earth, was not the sort of community to appear hospitable to a merchant group interested in widening its contacts and markets in the world at large. And while profits and personal welfare, in theory, might be more easily attained in a non-regulated world, the realities of the emerging imperial structure led some merchants to believe it was better to "do business" within the imperial limitations than obstinately to attempt to rebuild the older version of the society.

Given such circumstances, Governor Andros could have solicited allies upon whom to erect the Dominion of New England, but his own lack of political sense, and the sudden toppling of his king in England, proved too much for him and his regime. The news of the Glorious Revolution at home was all the signal needed by the Bay people. They soon had Andros in prison, a manifesto justifying their "revolution" issued, and the colony, as an interim device, returned to its former political structure.

David Lovejoy, in his introduction to "The Glorious Revolution in America" in Leonard W. Levy and Merrill D. Peterson (eds.), *Major Crises in American History* (1962), has suggested that "the overturning of governments in Massachusetts, New York, and Maryland had origins deeper than Stuart tyranny, the threat of Catholicism, and fear of the French and Indians. Local conflicts and cleavages, intensifying the crisis, doubtless had more to do with the rebellions in America than a change of monarchs in England."

Yet, despite the historians' recent concern with the internal structure of colonial society in the later seventeenth century, all are aware that the frictions between the colonies and England, generated by the imperial regulations and consolidations (particularly the creation of the Dominion of New England), were an essential element in most of these American "revolutions." In a much more direct sense than Bacon's Rebellion, the hostility in Massachusetts to the Andros program of tightening controls on commerce, instituting Anglican church services, re-examination of land titles, helped create the climax of the rebellion.

Similarly, the affairs in another part of the Dominion combined hostility to the formation of the new regime and local disruptions resulting from the social disorganization of the times. The "Glorious Revolution" in New York was to prove more bloody than the events in Massachusetts had been. Yet Lawrence Leder, who analyzes the Leisler Revolt in New York, in *Robert Livingston and the Politics of Colonial New York, 1654–1728* (1961), is impressed with patterns similar to those found in Massachusetts. It was not, in his view, a class struggle in the sense of the "haves" against the "have nots" that gave rise to the events that brought Jacob Leisler to the leadership of New York affairs after the collapse of the Dominion government. Nor was it that simple a division that accounts for the harshness of the reaction to Leisler's assumption of power (including the execution of Leisler and his lieutenant, Jacob Milborne) by the forces of a "restored" aristocracy. Rather than seeing Leisler as the leader of the downtrodden lower class, eagerly breaking the restraints around them, Leder's analysis emphasizes the basic collision as one between aristocrats and would-be aristocrats, between a relatively small group who wielded power and another relatively small group who wanted to take over that power.

But, again, the course of Empire did not rest solely on the internal factions or the results of their contests. Contributing to the developments in New York, as in Massachusetts, was the reaction of Americans to the consolidating attempts of James II, and the fall of the Dominion in New York, as in Massachusetts, disrupted this most extreme effort by England to order its northern colonies more completely and more rigidly into the orbit of Empire.

The trio of uprisings in America that at least partly occurred because of the radical events in England in 1688–1689 was completed by an episode in the proprietary of Maryland. Here, as in neighboring Virginia during the previous decade, it is more difficult to see the new imperial regulations as a major element in the origins of rebellion. Rather, internal conditions within Maryland itself were the primary ingredients in the explosion—the long-standing antagonisms between Catholic and Protestant settlers, the seemingly unshakable policy of the proprietor of maintaining a Catholic governing group in office, the feudal-type land-holding and inadequate Indian policies. The rebellion, when it came, fed on fears of an attempt by the deposed James II to establish a beach-head of Catholicism within Maryland. Together these elements led the Protestant Association, headed by John Coode, to crush the proprietary regime and create an interim structure to serve as Maryland's government until the new monarchs' will was known.

Thus, as of 1689–1690, the decades of imperial planning, the movement toward consolidation and regulation, had ended in a strange way. While Carolina and Virginia remained largely untouched by the events of the Glorious Revolution, every other mainland American province was now in an awkward state. All of those former governments encompassed within the short-lived Dominion of New England, as well as the deposed proprietary of Maryland and its neighbor, Pennsylvania (for William Penn's relations with James II, along with other charges, were used by his enemies to shear him of his proprietary rights), remained in an unsettled condition, awaiting the decisions that William III might make about his overseas possessions.

RESHAPING THE EMPIRE

Restructuring the empire was one of the many problems facing the new Protestant monarch of England after the Glorious Revolution. Since William III had accepted the English throne partly because he planned to bring that kingdom to the aid of the League of Augsburg in its military contest against Louis XIV of France, the affairs of England now took on a military cast. Establishing himself in his new kingdom and preparing for war in Europe absorbed most of the new king's energies; colonial problems necessarily were considered only as domestic and European affairs allowed. But in time William and his advisers turned to the two major questions posed by the revolutionary events in the colonies. There was, first, the question of over-all imperial structure—whether the basic aims of Empire as they had developed in the previous decades were to be altered, continued, expanded. And then, in a more specialized sense, it was necessary to consider the constitutional structure of each of those mainland colonies whose actions in the past months had ended the legitimately constituted government and which must be returned, in one fashion or another, to some stable arrangement.

The answer to the first of these questions demonstrated the deep-seated commitment of the English people to the basic tenets of mercantilistic thought which had brought the imperial structure as far as it was by the time of the Glorious Revolution. As the Restoration in 1660 had not altered the basic structure begun during the Cromwellian years, so now the exchange of the throne from James II to William III brought no alteration in the aims of the Empire. In fact, given the sudden turning in foreign policy to direct contest with France, strategic benefits of the Empire took on additional significance, extending the drive for imperial controls beyond the economic and social motivations of the past.

Two specific actions within the decade following the Glorious Revolution demonstrated these continued commitments to Empire. In England, the committee of the Privy Council responsible for supervision of colonial affairs, the Lords of Trade, was replaced by William with a new agency called the Board of Trade. Established as a combination of high-ranking noblemen and colonial experts, this fifteen-man board took over the functions of the older agency and became, at least in theory, the central agency for administering colonial affairs. At about the same time the structure of the Empire was further defined by Parliament in the comprehensive Navigation Act of 1696. This legislation continued the basic regulations of previous statutes and looked forward to more efficient enforcement of those laws with specific requirements for registration of commercial vessels, oaths from all colonial governors promising vigilant administration of the laws of trade, and the establishment of vice-admiralty courts within the colonies. These courts would provide opportunity for trials of accused violators outside the regular colonial courts, away from jury trials by neighbors reluctant to convict their fellow colonists for infringements of the imperial regulations.

On the other question—the re-establishment of legitimate governments within the individual colonies—William's decisions can be classed as rather middle-of-the-road settlements. The extreme alternatives which he might have considered ranged from, on the one hand, allowing the re-establishment of quasi-independent communities such as had existed before the Restoration in 1660 and, on the other hand, another attempt to institute consolidated government in America, perhaps another Dominion of New England. Instead of selecting either of these alternatives, William moved in the direction of composing relationships approximating those of the mid-1670's, thereby ensuring a perpetuation of the mixed and various structures which had earlier characterized the American plantations. While there would continue to be impulses toward uniformity, especially a determination to reduce all of the colonies to royal status, for the moment (and certainly partly as a result of the military necessities of that war period) the Crown was content to allow a basic reversion to older arrangements.

This meant that the reconstituted governments in each of the mainland American colonies would be formed on the basis of its past history, in an individual way. New Hampshire would revert to its form when created in 1679, a province on the model of Virginia, with a royally appointed governor and council and an elected lower house of assembly. Rhode Island and Connecticut, emerging from the defunct Dominion, contended that their post-Restoration charters were still valid. Successful in their claims, they were restored as corporate, chartered communities. Massachusetts also waged a vigorous defense of its rights to its old charter, but without success. Imperial considerations, and past history, necessitated some alterations and the result was a new charter, issued in 1691.

Massachusetts, under its new patent, would have a royally appointed governor and a council composed in a unique fashion, with the members nominated by the elected lower house of assembly, subject to confirmation by the governor. The franchise in the province now was to rest on property, rather than religious, qualifications. Legislation of the Massachusetts General Court was subject to review and possible disallowance by the Crown. The arrangements were something of a compromise, mid-way between the desires of the Massachusetts people to return to their 1629 charter and the suggestions of those in England who argued for a total reduction of the province to royal status.

New York, set free from proprietary and Dominion control, was made a royal province on the Virginia model, with appointed governor and council and, after long years without the privilege, an elected lower house of assembly. The other part of the former Dutch conquest, now severed from the original proprietors and in the hands of capitalist landlords, would be created the royal province of New Jersey shortly after the turn of the century.

The drive to reduce the Penn and Calvert proprietaries met a varied, but ultimately similar, end. William Penn was deprived of his governing rights in Pennsylvania for two years (1692–1694), but he regained his chartered powers, and he and his heirs would retain those rights, although not uncontested, until the time of the American Revolution. In Maryland, the story extended further in time. William III decided to take over the Calverts' political authority and did so, allowing the economic benefits of the proprietary to remain in Calvert control. This arrangement would last until 1715. Then the political rights were restored to the proprietor.

Virginia's structure had not been upset by the events of the time, and the Old Dominion needed no specific reorganization. For the moment the same was true of the Carolina proprietary. Later, in the coming century, the rights of seven of the eight grantees were purchased by the Crown (the eighth received a special grant of lands in North Carolina), and Carolina, by then divided permanently into its northern and southern parts, became royal provinces. As for the borderlands south of Carolina, it was not until the 1730's that the effort to erect the outpost called Georgia got underway.

By the end of the seventeenth century, then, the Empire had been put back together after its humpty-dumpty-like fall. In the first six decades of the century ahead, the English would pursue their national goals, building internal strength, waging expensive but ultimately victorious warfare on France and other enemies, and directing the affairs of the Empire in such a way that the goals of domestic well-being, security, and prestige were all furthered. And in America, during those same six decades, the colonists would experience economic, population, social, and cultural growth, emerging at the end of the era as something unique in world experience—a new people, operating within unique techniques of social organization. But at no time during those first six decades of the eighteenth century did England ever systematically attempt to reshape the Empire to conform with the consolidated, uniform system that remained the "theoretical" Empire in the minds of some Englishmen, including many charged with administering imperial affairs. Rather, an ever-widening division grew between the theories of empire as they had been defined in the seventeenth century and the actual working realities of relationships between parent state and colonies as they developed in the century that followed.

TWO

The Economic
Empire

Of all aspects of the first British Empire, no other has so concerned American historians as the economic regulations of the old imperial system, and especially those aspects codified in the laws known as the Acts of Trade and Navigation. A description of those laws has satisfied some historians as a description of the imperial connection between colonies and mother country. For other students of America's early years, an evaluation of the effect of those laws upon colonial development has been sufficient to characterize the general effects of imperial ties with Great Britain. The one central question that has long engaged the historians' curiosity and talents concerning the origins of the United States has been: How did the British imperial system affect the American colonies? Were the economic regulations an obvious example of British "tyranny" over freedom-seeking Americans, as George Bancroft asserted in the nineteenth century? Or was the first British Empire, economically, a well-balanced, reciprocal arrangement, in which the colonies as well as the mother country prospered, as George L. Beer, Charles M. Andrews, and other "imperialist" historians writing in the late nineteenth and early twentieth centuries stated? Are such "imperialists" wrong in their pleasant pictures of mutual benefits, as Louis Hacker and other historians of the 1930's and 1940's asserted, emphasizing instead the competitive nature of the British mercantile capitalists and their counterparts within the colonies? Or are the more recent evaluations of Oliver M. Dickerson and Lawrence H. Gipson—who see the Americans peculiarly blessed by the economic and other advantages derived from the imperial connection—closer to historical truth?

Before turning to the specific question of the impact of the Empire upon colonial life, certain more general facets of the imperial relationship need to be described, so that a proper perspective may be maintained when considering the more specific question. Otherwise, some of the more significant aspects of the economic empire will be forgotten or misleadingly reduced in importance.

First it should be noted that, in addition to imperial regulation, many other elements entered into the composition of the developing colonial economy, including such various and relative elements as the availability of investment capital, the supply and cost of labor, the constantly shifting economic climate produced by war-time or peace-time needs, the expanding population of the colonies, and the changing endeavors to utilize profitably the natural resources of the colonies. Unless all of these and at times other variables are included in an evaluation, historically misleading conclusions may result from any attempt to interpret the significance of imperial regulation.

Second, the most obvious, direct impact of imperial regulation in the colonies was apparent in the mercantile and industrial life, yet the colonial economies were based, in very large measure, not upon commerce directly, but rather upon agriculture. The overwhelming majority of Americans, perhaps some 90 per cent of the total population, earned its daily sustenance directly from agricultural endeavors. In the pattern of the economic life of each individual colonist, mercantile activities (as well as the few nascent industries and such extractive enterprises as fur gathering and lumbering and fishing) were less directly related to the daily struggle for survival than the production of agricultural goods. Thus it is of some significance that, although indirectly the imperial economic system and agriculture were intertwined, the impact of the trade laws could be experienced directly by only a limited fraction of the total colonial population.

Given the overriding significance of agriculture in the colonial economies, the patterns established and operated for securing and holding real estate become central to any analysis of the economic development of those colonial societies. While exceptions to the rule may be cited here and there, for the most part land acquisition was not an imperially regulated enterprise in the eighteenth century. There were sectional and regional differences in the way in which private individuals gained and held agricultural land, but generally the entire procedure was locally (that is, provincially) controlled. In the seventeenth century, while vast proprietary grants were being patented and provincial governments structured, imperial decisions often directly affected land-holding. But in the eighteenth century, as governments became stabilized and, except for Georgia, the major severances of the Crown's domains had been accomplished, there was less and less opportunity for any blueprint for land acquisition to be imposed. The provincial governments, whether chartered, proprietary, or royal, devised their own operations for land granting, and the ease or difficulty of obtaining land titles depended primarily upon the dominant political group's intentions and objectives. While it is true that in the plantation colonies of the south, particularly in South Carolina and Virginia, and in the former Dutch province of New York, large estates worked against the characteristics, the basic pattern of land-holding in British North America was one of small holdings, individually cultivated, upon relatively free tenure. It was this fact that made the British colonies the dream of so many immigrants of the eighteenth century. In contrast to the world they knew in Britain, in Ireland, or on the continent of Europe, America was a limitless expanse of productive agricultural land, where the self-sufficient individual might attain goals of personal welfare forever closed to him in the land-poor Old World.

This promise, actually obtainable in the colonies, was in only minor ways directly interfered with by official British actions. During the years before 1763, in fact, if there was an official British policy concerning land acquisition, it was often directed toward a continuation and advancement of small land-holding. The imposition of quit rents (annual fees levied without regard to improvements upon land held of the king or proprietor) were encouraged by Britain for, in addition to their obvious advantage as revenue producers, they tended to discourage acquisition of or speculation in large, unimproved tracts of land. Working in counter-direction, it is true, the grants, late in the era, of trans-Appalachian lands to syndicates or land companies tended to further the opposite trend. But, in balance, British imperial regulations or, in most instances, the lack of them, allowed the widespread holding of real property in the colonies and the shaping of a society characterized by "middle-class" agriculturalists.

While of much less concern to historians than other facets of mercantilism, Curtis P. Nettels (*The Roots of American Civilization*, 2d ed., 1963) has pointed out that, in so far as such a policy existed, the concept of small land-holdings did complement the basic tenets of mercantilism, for the production of goods from small holdings would increase and enlarge commerce and thus work to advance the trade of the Empire. Land in small lots, diligently cultivated, prospered commerce, while land in large, unsettled tracts, held speculatively until social needs pushed values upward, contributed little or nothing to trade. The British policy of encouraging the peopling of the colonies—first from Britain and later from the continent of

Europe—worked toward the same ends, for large populations in the dominions would increase the trade of the Empire and further develop the national strength. Until about the 1680's English mercantilist thought had pronounced emigration from the homeland to the colonies a blessing, for it siphoned excess labor from England. But later, analysis of the home economy brought a change. Fearing too much weakening of the home labor force from such emigration, the imperialists now stressed the advantages of immigration into America from continental Europe and from the more mature American colonies into the newer settlements. In both instances, however, the goal was the same, and the spectacular increases in colonial population during the eighteenth century attested to the success of the policy of encouragement—a policy indicated by various decisions and instructions from the Board of Trade and the Parliamentary legislation which stipulated relatively easy naturalization of alien immigrants.

Imperial planners also became involved in attempts to shape colonial economic ventures in a complementary rather than competitive place in the Empire. In an entirely natural way, British imperial theorists saw benefits from colonies producing goods unavailable in the homeland, thus reducing dependence upon other nations for needed or desired goods. The list of such products ranged from sugar and cotton to tobacco, rice, and indigo, to naval stores and ship timbers, wine, and silk. The records of the imperial economic planning contain widely differing results. In some instances, notably indigo and naval stores, the policies were quite successful, as will be noted in greater detail later. Other experiments, especially the efforts to stimulate wine and silk culture, ended as discouraging failures. No amount of imperial prodding, it seems, could overcome more powerful determinants, such as the scarcity of laborers skilled in those enterprises and, perhaps even more significant, the fact that greater, quicker, and more certain returns could be predicted from other agricultural endeavors.

It made little difference whether or not the originators of a colony intended it that way; the events of the early years in most of the mainland plantations demonstrated that permanence and stability could be assured only by a colony's ability to sustain itself through local food production. Dependence upon a home base in England for supplies proved much too hazardous. Thus agricultural production, in its earliest form, was directed to crops needed to sustain the newly planted outpost. Only after the colony's immediate needs were satisfied was time and energy available to develop exportable surpluses.

But, having satisfied those initial needs, the American colonies could, and did, move into the more advanced state of production, harvesting surpluses which, in turn, required transportation to increasingly far-spread markets. Thus agriculture, in its secondary stage in the colonies, generated the commercial sector of the economy. Commerce, it is true, had been evolving through impetus from fur trading and from fishing and, to a lesser extent, lumbering, for all of those extractive enterprises had produced cargoes for extracolonial markets. It was, however, the success of the Americans in expanding their farms and plantations that formed the basic foundations for the general expansion of the colonial economy during the eighteenth century, coupled as it was with the Americans' ability to seek out and develop markets in which to dispose profitably of those agricultural products. And it is at this point, when agricultural goods entered into the commerce outside the colony of production, that the colonists were brought most directly into contact with the commercial regulations of the Empire, spelled out in the Acts of Trade and Navigation.

SHIPPING AND STAPLES

As stated at the beginning of this chapter, the question of the impact of the Navigation Acts upon the American colonial economy has been a favorite topic for analysis, discussion, and argument among historians for many years. There are several reasons why this has been so. For one thing, the topic is, to some extent, a central question in any attempt to assess motivations for the American Revolution, and the search for answers to the question of the significance of economic regulation after 1763 has drawn historians backward into the colonial era, seeking antecedents of the policies of the mother country, and American reactions to those policies, of the Revolutionary years. Another reason undoubtedly underlying much of the interest in the problem is the fact that throughout the years since the Americans left the British Empire, debate over specific commercial policies and general national economic regulations has flourished. These debates have ranged from the nineteenth century debates over free trade to American contests over tariff policies; from Panama Canal regulations to the European Common Market. In all of these debates, "history" has been sought as a weapon in the arguments to prove virtues or defects of regulated commercial systems.

It is probably also true that a study of imperial trade regulations, at least in the less sophisticated definitions, is in some ways easier to engage in, less abstract in definition and involving data seemingly more manageable, than some other aspects of the first British Empire. The trade laws, in basic form, were statutes of Parliament, words capable of scholarly analysis. Revenue receipts were recorded; port entrances and clearances, as well as merchants' papers, survive to be studied. Compared with concepts which are more difficult to define, such as (to cite only a single example), the "psychology" of a colonial population, the economic Empire may be examined with more ordinary tools of scholarship. Yet it is interesting that Lawrence A. Harper ("The Effect of the Navigation Acts on the Thirteen Colonies" in Richard B. Morris (ed.), *The Era of the American Revolution,* 1939), after concluding that the colonists paid a "heavy price" under the system for the benefits they received from Britain (a conclusion, incidentally, emphatically rejected by other scholars), cautioned against assuming that this automatically implied that the trade laws were a major determinant in the American decision to revolt against British rule. As Harper warned, any simple "cost accounting, balance sheet" (the words are mine, not his) approach to the question alone may be historically misleading, for regardless of what modern computers may tell us about the cost of imperial connection, the colonists might well, and in Harper's view did, act from their own interpretations of what they (not we) believed and experienced. The Empire existed for more than three generations before American resistance created the crisis of revolution. Harper reminds us that human beings learn, over a long period of time, to live under many undesirable or unprofitable restraints. Statistical, customs-house history alone can never tell us with precision what the actual historical impact of imperial membership brought. Most students of the American colonies and the British Empire have been aware of the limitations Harper warns against, and have cast their historical search-nets widely. Yet a surprising number of studies of the question have been, and probably always will be, predicated on the primacy of the significance of statistical analysis, emphasizing the "costs" and "dividends" of the imperial connection. One such attempt is Robert Paul Thomas, "A Quantitative Approach to the Study of the Effects of British Imperial Policy upon Colonial Welfare: Some Preliminary Findings," *The Journal of Economic History,* XXV (December 1965). The models Thomas uses are the estimated annual averages for the period 1763–1772 and for the single year 1770; he ventures the hypothesis that "membership in the British Empire, after 1763, did not impose a significant hardship upon the American colonies." Although this relates to years beyond the limits of this book, similar studies might yield similar findings for earlier decades.

In turning to an actual examination of what historians have concluded from their investigations of the nature of the economic empire, it is necessary also to caution against an either-or, black-white interpretation. Most modern scholars concede that, in over-all assessment, the imperial regulations Britain instituted were neither totally harmful nor totally beneficial to America, but that within the wide regions between such extreme characterizations is to be found the proper assessment. Of course, in attempting to locate the precise point within that "middle ground" historians have disagreed and do disagree.

The departure point for a general examination of the problem might well be the findings of Oliver M. Dickerson who, in 1951, reported the conclusions of a detailed investigation of the old colonial system in a book entitled *The Navigation*

Acts and the American Revolution (1951). Building on, but revising and modifying previous findings, particularly those of George L. Beer and Lawrence A. Harper, Dickerson addressed himself to the central question: How oppressive were the Navigation Acts? The answers which he found to that question form the first half of his book. His findings are buttressed both by specific, detailed analyses of the trade laws in operation and by his study of the attitudes of American colonists toward those laws. In general, he reports little in the system to condemn. He sees the American colonies as prospering under the aegis of the British Empire; he views the imperial regulations as reciprocally beneficial to mother country and colonies; he reports negatively on his search for significant displays of American hostility to the imperial system; and he concludes that, until 1763, the colonists lived in, if not the best of all economic worlds, at least a very good one, in which both they and their parent state developed increasing prosperity. Far from interfering with this happy scene, the economic regulations were what prompted it: "For one hundred years," Dickerson asserts, "the trade and navigation system had provided the most important cement of empire."

Dickerson's method of analysis is to examine the effects of the Navigation Acts, piece by piece, upon the colonies, arriving in the end at the general conclusions summarized in the preceding paragraph. He begins with the Navigation Act of 1660, and finds that whatever adverse effects that legislation had generated during its first four decades was no longer a serious concern after 1700. This was the Parliamentary Act which restricted the carrying trade of the Empire to English and English-colonial vessels. Initially, at least, it had created a shortage of ships to handle the American produce; for foreign competitors, especially the Dutch, had been driven from the commerce and there were not enough English vessels to fill the vacuum created. In the past, some scholars have charged that this freight shortage both increased freight rates and hampered the natural expansion of the American economy, presumably throughout most, if not all, of the colonial era. This condition, if it existed, certainly would have constituted a significantly oppressive feature of regulation. But Dickerson answers that any such shortage of freight capacity had been fully taken care of by the beginnings of the eighteenth century; thus that part of the 1660 Act did not affect freight rates after 1700.

Instead of seeing the 1660 Act as harmful or oppressive to the colonists, Dickerson concludes that it actually helped the growth of the American economy in two distinct ways. First, it enhanced shipbuilding in the New World, for vessels built in the colonies (or owned and operated there) classified as English ships within the definitions of the statute. In fact, Dickerson believes that this was directly responsible for the rising colonial shipbuilding industry, an industry which produced, by the time of the American Revolution, one-third of the tonnage of ships registered under the British flag. Dickerson's enthusiasm is somewhat tempered by other historians who have pointed out that closer examination reveals that most of the American vessels were small sloops and schooners, used largely in coastal and West Indian commerce, while the bulk of the trans-Atlantic trade continued to be carried in the larger vessels built in Britain. This specialization in ship construction somewhat reduces the beneficial aspects of the Act of 1660 as Dickerson describes it. For he asserts that the only colonial region which could "theoretically" have found the limitation of the carrying trade to British vessels "even an imaginary grievance" were the plantation areas, because after 1700 English, and particularly New England, shipping expanded so that there was ample capacity and competition for cargoes. But if the colonial-built shipping did not carry a large part of the trans-Atlantic trade, then the expansion of ship construction which answered the freight requirements of the southern provinces was British, not American. Even so, the development of the shipbuilding industry in the colonies is impressive, and the Act of 1660 helped to make it so.

Dickerson sees a second positive benefit from the legislation in its elimination of the hazards and uncertainties that foreign shipping would have created in the colonial economy, especially because of the many years of international warfare during the eighteenth century. Since the colonists were dependent upon overseas markets for their prosperity, chaos that might have resulted from dependence on foreign shippers was eliminated. Stability, a requisite for economic development, was attained. War disrupted colonial commercial and, indirectly, agricultural and industrial life much less than it would have if "alien" carriage in peacetime had been allowed. As it was, British and colonial ships could continue their freight hauling, usually along trade lanes protected by the British navy. Thus Dickerson denies any burdensome result from the carrying clauses of the Act of 1660, arguing instead that colonial shipbuilding prospered and American commerce was stabilized as a result of the beneficial policy.

A second feature of the Navigation Act of 1660 (and later additions to that legislation) that Dickerson investigates is the policy of enumeration—that is, the designation of certain staple colonial products for shipment only to markets within the British Empire. If enumerated, the product had to be traded from its colony of origin to imperial ports, even though, in some cases, most of the goods eventually were reshipped to foreign consumer markets. There were three major products of the mainland colonies that were enumerated: tobacco, rice, and indigo. These products, Dickerson states, did not have to be grown anywhere, yet the fact that they formed the economic base of the colonial American south indicates that, even though enumerated, they were profitable—more profitable, probably, than alternative, unenumerated goods which the colonists might have produced. The choice, he explains, was up to the Americans. The fact that they continued to concentrate on enumerated products suggests that the market restrictions on them could not have been a controlling factor, oppressive to the colonists.

Considering each of these products individually, Dickerson first examines the tobacco industry. He reports that the production of tobacco in the Chesapeake region was an enterprise full of risks and difficulties, but rather than linking these hazards with enumeration, he asserts that the basic problem was the same problem "commercial farmers" always face—the perennial, chronic condition of being in debt. Despite this, he views the tobacco industry as basically prosperous, up to the time of the American Revolution. This, he says, was true not just of the tobacco planters, but of the entire economic structure that was hinged on the product—the shippers, the merchants, the financiers, as well as the planters. In fact, he says, the proof of the benefits the structure dispensed can be seen in what happened to the industry after the Revolution, when for three-quarters of a century the American tobacco industry struggled to regain the stability and prosperity it had known as part of the British Empire. The heart of this system was the central British market, providing a focal point for the entire industry, bringing a needed, responsible measure of order to the American (production) side, the British (transportation, distribution, and financial) side, and for that large part of the product which was reshipped from Britain, to the continental European (consumer) side of the enterprise.

Not all historians would agree with this singularly pleasant picture of the colonial tobacco economy. Some scholars suggest that the American side of the industry declined in vigor during the closing years of the colonial era; that the tobacco region's vitality had weakened, despite the gloss of luxurious, credit-based living. They point to the increased tempo of agricultural diversification in both Virginia and Maryland as indicators of the tobacco planters' need to find stability in a more varied economic foundation, turning to wheat, hemp, and other crops to supplement their tobacco earnings. But diversification attempts were not limited to the last years of the old Empire; resistance to and unhappiness with the concentration on tobacco are long-tenured elements in the Chesapeake history. And the impetus for diversification often came from Britain, not the colonies. Despite this, tobacco remained "king," and with it British merchants flourished, Crown revenues increased, and the American planters made money.

Some critics might say: Even if all this was true, wouldn't the Americans have made *more* money if they had been free to trade their tobacco outside the Empire—if tobacco, unregulated, had been freed from enumeration and the crushing burdens of imperial duties, merchants' charges of warehousing and commissions for handling, especially since a large part of the crop was ultimately peddled in non-British markets? Not true, says Dickerson. The Americans could not have created a central market to replace that which existed in the British Isles. From this market came the benefits of capital financing and credit arrangements, experienced wholesaling, the general "know how" essential to the entire industry. The proof, again, is visible in the disorganized condition of the American tobacco enterprises after the American Revolution. As far as tobacco is concerned (and it was by far the single most significant economic enterprise within the mainland colonies), Dickerson is positive that membership in the Empire brought benefits far outweighing any burdens imposed by regulation.

Much the same patterns are visible in the rice industry, where again the world market (at least the *western* world market) was located in Great Britain, to which the enumerated rice from America was sent. In this case, however, the colonials had been allowed a dispensation; the rice of Carolina and Georgia could be shipped directly to Mediterranean ports south of Cape Finisterre. Even so, according to Dickerson, more than half as much American rice was imported into southern Europe through the English market as was brought directly from America, demonstrating the value of that central market. When the Revolution later eliminated the market in Britain and with it the financial benefits available to American planters, the rice industry of the United States lost the flourishing health it had known and rapidly declined.

The third staple crop from the mainland colonies that was enumerated was indigo. It was not only enumerated, but was officially encouraged by the payment of a bounty on its export from the colonies to Britain. This vegetable derivative, so useful as a dye in the textile industry, had been developed in South Carolina during the eighteenth century and would prosper there until the American Revolution. Then, as in the case of rice and tobacco, separation from the Empire ended the profitableness of indigo because, Dickerson explains, the imperial bounty was used to encourage the industry in other parts of the Empire, creating competition against which the American industry could not survive. Thus he sees this third major staple enterprise dependent upon its imperial encouragement, and while the advantages Britain gained from her policies are not denied, the story of colonial indigo is a prize exhibit demonstrating the benefits of the Empire to the colonists.

THE NORTHERN COMMERCE

The enumerated products of major importance to the mainland colonies were all southern in origin. Because they formed the bulk of raw exports desired by the mother country, they placed those plantation provinces in what imperial planners considered an ideal situation. Not only did they directly answer the needs of the nation; their annual shipments of goods to Britain provided the means whereby the southern colonists could purchase the fabricated goods which flowed back across the Atlantic each year. This trade was also regulated. The Staple Act of 1663 provided that goods imported into the colonies, either of English or northern European origin, must be cleared through an English port. While the charges for handling these shipments in England increased the ultimate price to the consumer in the colony, the southern provinces, with their yearly credits for their staple crops sent to England, could live and evidently prosper within the regulations. But the northern colonists, lacking the type of exportable products needed in the homeland, faced a different situation.

The middle provinces, with their diversified agricultural surpluses, including increasing quantities of grain products, and the New England colonies both produced competitive, not complementary exports. For these there was no regular market at home, and in order to develop their internal economies and to meet the necessary payments for fabricated goods imported from England (as the law required), markets in other parts of the world had to be developed. That the northern colonists were able to find such markets, and to maintain and further their prosperity within the framework of imperial regulation, indicates something of the imaginative talents of those northern colonists. The need led to the development of intercolonial trading, to the opening and expanding of markets in southern Europe, and, above all, to the increasingly influential traffic between the northern mainland ports and the West Indian islands. Only by developing those markets were the northern merchants able to accumulate balances of profit sufficient to continue the importation of desired goods from England.

In his study of the Navigation Acts, Dickerson acknowledges the significance of this trade, but he cautions about treating the separate areas of commerce as compartmentalized units, worrying about balances within each bilateral set of exchanges. Rather, he presents the alternative of viewing the total imperial trade as a single unit and asserts that within this sort of frame, both the mother country and the colonists prospered during the era.

While there is much to be said for this way of looking at the effects of regulation, there are some unanswered questions too. If the restrictions on importation of goods directly from England had not been imposed, might not the northern colonies have found satisfactory markets in a less hazardous way? Might not those markets have allowed their own agriculture and industry to develop more quickly and more fully? Certainly central to the forces shaping the patterns of the northern colonial commerce was the essential need to garner the credits to pay for goods imported from England. And, although through ingenuity and hard work the northern merchants managed to make profits from commerce within the regulations, perhaps they might have advanced more fully if such roundabout commercial patterns had not been required.

Then too, while it may satisfy twentieth-century historians to view the imperial trade in its totality and to seek the broader picture of all imperial commerce within one frame, it is quite obvious that some of the contemporary merchants and policy makers lacked that perspective in their own time. No matter how clearly today's scholar can see the interrelationships between the various segments of imperial commerce, to merchants and politicians then such connections were often obscured. A good example of this is the official attitude of Britain toward the increasing commerce between the northern colonies and the foreign West Indies.

The elements of this trade may be described, in their simplest form, in this manner: The Caribbean islands which produced sugar and its byproducts were possessed by various European powers; some were English, some were French, some Dutch, some Spanish. In their search for markets, northern mainland merchants had found these islands a place of profit. Single-crop areas, the islands particularly needed foodstuffs to feed their laboring force and timber products (barrels and casks) to package their export sugar products. Fish, beef and pork, staves, hoops and barrel heads could be taken from the northern mainland ports to the islands and exchanged for sugar, molasses, and specie. The last two were most important. The molasses was returned to the rum distilleries in the colonies; the specie produced the means of paying for goods imported from England.

Thus, upon this trade with the West Indies much of the prosperity of the northern mainland colonies depended. It was obvious to many northern merchants, as it is to historians today, that any diminution of this trade would necessarily imperil the continued volume of imports from the mother country. Yet on occasion British imperial policy seemed to allow no genuine appreciation of this fact. When war erupted between European powers, British officials insisted that trade between the mainland colonies and the foreign islands be halted. There might have been no problem had the British islands been able to absorb the mainland cargoes and satisfy the demand of the northern merchants for sugar products. But they could not, and thus the trade encompassed the French and other foreign islands. Trading with the enemy was looked upon in England in its narrowest sense as an act of disloyalty, without (Americans claimed) full appreciation of the hazards to the imperial economy a disruption of such trading would entail.

Even more obvious, in Americans' eyes, as an indicator of the lack of comprehension of the ways the imperial trade actually flowed was the Parliamentary enactment in 1733 of the legislation known as the Molasses Act. This was a peace-time measure, legislated in response to demands from the British West Indian sugar interests for protection against the competition they faced from the foreign islands. It imposed unreasonably heavy duties upon foreign sugar products imported into the mainland colonies. To American mainlanders, it signified a sacrifice of their economic well-being for the economic security of the British islands.

Some historians, including Lawrence Henry Gipson (*The British Empire before the American Revolution,* 1936 to date), defend British action here by stressing the relative importance of the West Indies to Britain, compared with the lesser significance of the mainland colonies. It is also true that, in practice, the act was never enforced. Commerce in sugar products between foreign islands and the northern ports continued. In fact, Dickerson claims that even the British sugar interests in the West Indies did not desire enforcement of the Act. But Gilman Ostrander ("The Colonial Molasses Trade," *Agricultural History,* XXX [April 1956]) believes the effects of the legislation were harmful to the colonies on the mainland, for the Act limited the expansion of their search for trade and markets, and it arbitrarily attempted to sacrifice the profits of one part of the Empire for the benefit of another.

Certainly the fact that the legislation was enacted should not be ignored in any general review of British imperial legislation, no matter how minimal its actual effect in shaping colonial commerce. For the very enactment indicates that, at best, the total pattern of imperial trade was not completely clear to British policy makers or, and in some ways even more revealing in the light of the colonists' charges, the welfare of one part of the Empire might indeed be reduced in order to protect the interests of another part.

The generally accepted conclusion that the Molasses Act of 1733 never was effectively enforced leads directly to the larger question: How rigidly were all of the Navigation Acts administered? Evidence gathered, and interpretation drawn from that evidence, again seems to differ. One group of historians has been convinced that evasion of the trade laws was an almost full-time occupation of the American colonists. They paint the trade laws as almost entirely lacking in real significance. In this view, the Americans continued to conduct commerce as they wished, without let or hindrance. In fact, scholars like George L. Beer, who probably would have agreed with the more recent evaluations like Dickerson's that the colonies flourished within the imperial structure, partly explained their opinions on the basis of the ineffectiveness of the laws in actual operation. An opposing view, shared by Dickerson and, earlier, Lawrence A. Harper (who believed that *for* this reason the laws might have been burdensome to the colonists), suggests the opposite, asserting that the great majority of the American colonial trade was conducted within the channels set down by the trade laws, with only a few extralegal excursions, such as the practical nullification of the Molasses Act, occurring at those few points where compliance might have completely wrecked a segment of the colonial economy. Esmond Wright (*Fabric of Freedom: 1763–1800*, 1961) sums up this viewpoint, stating that tea and molasses were the only commodities systematically smuggled into mainland ports.

Thomas Barrow (*Trade and Empire: The British Customs Service in Colonial America*, 1967) is not so certain the matter can be dismissed that easily. His listing of smuggled items is more extended, including gunpowder, paper, and luxury items. He admits that illicit trade ". . . was in the nature of a supplement to regular trade, the merchants adjusting their activities to the needs and the profits of the moment. At no point, except possibly in the frantic moments preceding the outbreak of the Revolution, did illicit trade even approach the legitimate English trade in volume or value." But, writes Barrow, "The major importance of illicit trade lay not in its volume but in its effect. The evidence suggests that the colonial merchants were restrained from such activities by the economic advantages of trade with England rather than by enforcement of the laws. When evasion was profitable, it was usually possible; the colonists could indulge in it with relative freedom. The consequences were serious, since a general disrespect for law was a logical result."

Then too, perhaps what people thought was occurring was as important, perhaps at times even more important, than what was actually happening. It seems that, at least on occasion, some of those men in Britain responsible for planning and executing colonial policies assumed that Americans generally, and New Englanders in particular, operated outside the law on every possible occasion; that smuggling had become a distinctive American trait; and that this "fact" needed to be considered in all planning concerning the regulation of the imperial trade.

INDUSTRIAL REGULATIONS

Besides the regulation of commerce within the Empire, to ensure that strategic materials were not lost to foreign states and that the flow of goods within the Empire protected the national interests, Britain also laid down a series of regulations concerning industrial development within the American provinces. Some of these measures were intended to discourage the entrance of colonists into sectors of the economy where they would provide unwanted competition to home industries. Others were designed to encourage particular activities which would enhance the national interests by reducing Britain's dependence upon other parts of the world for desired or necessary commodities.

The way in which such imperial regulations were turned to the industry of indigo has been described above. At least some historians believe that the industry's prosperity rested upon the bounties paid by Britain. Something of the same sort of encouragement was given to those items which were directly used by the merchants in their sailing vessels and by the royal naval fleet: ship timbers, masts, naval stores, and hemp. The need for developing sources of these commodities rested upon two situations. The timber available in Britain for shipbuilding, especially the tall, broad trees needed for masts in sailing vessels, was rapidly being depleted, and a new source was required. Naval stores—that is, pitch, tar, turpentine, and resin—all products of pitch pine forests, Britain ordinarily secured from the Baltic area, but reliance upon this foreign source for strategic materials created hazards, especially in war-time. American sources for naval materials not only would keep the trade within the Empire and further the goal of imperial self-sufficiency; a dangerous dependence upon foreign sources for vital materials would be eliminated.

The actual methods by which the goals of this policy were furthered differed from product to product. In the case of masts and ship timbers, a rudimentary conservation policy was established by which tracts of standing timber, particularly in New England's extensive white pine forests, were set aside. These "King's Woods" became forest reserves, from which, under contract, sanctioned cuttings could take place. Naval stores, on the other hand, were treated in a method similar to indigo, with bounties paid upon the exportation of American products to the homeland. The primary colonial source of naval stores was developed in North Carolina.

In addition to encouraging products like indigo and naval stores with direct bounties, the shape of the economic empire was also manipulated by restrictive legislation enacted in response to demands by specific interest groups within Britain who felt threatened by competition, actual or potential, from the American colonies. This type of regulation was specifically directed against three types of industrial products: woolen textiles, hats, and iron.

The earliest enactment of this sort was a law regulating woolens. Parliament, in 1699, attempted to reduce or eliminate competition to British woolen interests from both Irish and American producers. The law's impact was probably much greater in Ireland than in America, for there a developing textile industry posed an immediate threat to the English. It might, incidentally, be pointed out that there was a secondary effect of the law in Ireland. The depression of the industry there, following the imposition of the restrictions, was partly responsible for the immense emigration from northern Ireland to the American colonies in the eighteenth century.

In America, the effects of the legislation were less dramatic and probably less significant. The Woolens Act prohibited only the exportation of woolens by water from the place of production, so domestic, village, and even colony-wide commerce in locally made cloth was still permissible. But since, at the time of enactment, the colonial textile industry was still very much an infant industry, largely a domestic enterprise, at most the regulation could only keep a potential industry from developing. Whether, without the restrictions, a sizable colonial American woolen industry ever would have developed is uncertain. We have no thorough, recent investigation of the problem, but an older examination of the question by Victor S. Clark in *The History of Manufactures in the United States* (1929) concluded with a denial of the possibility of such development. Two basic elements seemed to work against it. Colonial labor was always a high-priced commodity, and it is doubtful if a textile industry could have attracted sufficient numbers of skilled workers. Also, as long as British woolens, which were superior products, could be obtained for lower prices than domestically made cloth, there was little reason to devote energy or capital to the colonial cloth industry. Thus, it is reasoned, the Woolens Act of 1699 had little actual effect on the development of the colonial economy.

The second industry to be regulated in a restrictive manner was the manufacture of hats. Again, the legislation (in 1732) was instigated by English manufacturers who feared the competition of American producers. In this case, the proscriptive legislation not only forbade the exportation of manufactured hats from the colony of origin by water; it also laid down rules restricting the number of apprentices in a hatmaking shop to no more than two and forbade contracting of Negro apprentices. And, unlike the Woolens Act, these restrictions on hat making involved an industry which consumed raw materials (North American furs) from sources much closer to colonial producers than to their competitors in England.

The effects of the legislation are debated by historians. Dickerson, for example, believes that, although there might have been what he terms a "temporary effect" on the development of an export trade in hats from New England, the overall effect was not serious, for it was "more advantageous" for hatmakers to move around the colonies, plying their trade from place to place, than it would have been for them to have established permanent shops and produced for markets from there. On the other hand, Lawrence A. Harper has calculated that, among all the industrial regulations, the Hat Act probably came closest to ruining a young American industry which was already reasonably well developed in the northern colonies. Before the enactment, New York and New England hatters were exporting their products to other parts of America and to Europe. In his view, the legislation restricted the natural development the American hat industry might otherwise have enjoyed. In this case, confronted with opposing expert interpretations, there is little choice but to examine the arguments more closely. Dickerson's assertion that hatmakers prospered more from a nomadic pursuit of their trade than they would have from fixed industrial locations is not further explained; he presents no specific evidence demonstrating economic advantages enjoyed by wandering hatmakers. Perhaps Harper's argument that the Hat Act was truly a burden to the colonial economy is closer to historical truth.

Finally, there were restrictions placed on the colonial iron industry which, like the woolens and hat regulations, had their origins in England among the iron interests who looked to Parliament for protection against colonial competition. We know more about this particular phase of British regulation than we do about others because of the studies by Arthur C. Bining, especially his findings reported in *The British Regulation of the Colonial Iron Industry* (1933). Bining traced with care the divergent forces in England interested in regulating the colonial iron industry—interests which divided into two basic groups. One side, the British producers of raw iron (pig and bar iron), were worried about competing with American producers of raw iron and wanted protection against them. On the other side, the users of raw iron, who fabricated it into finished products, were interested in developing sources of raw iron in America but, at the same time, wanted protection against American finished ironwares. Other indirectly related interests were also involved. The owners of woodlots in England, the coal producers, and others whose business connections with one or both sides of the British iron industry would be affected by regulatory legislation, became allies of the antagonists in the battle.

The struggle between British iron interests for protection eventually resulted in the Iron Act of 1750, a victory for the manufacturers of finished ironwares. The legislation encouraged American exportation of pig and bar iron to Britain by eliminating import duties on colonial raw iron there. But new slitting mills, rolling mills, tilt-hammer forges, and steel works were not to be erected in the provinces. The colonies would be producers of raw goods, not finished products.

Having traced the complicated origins of the Iron Act, Bining turned to examine the effects of the legislation in the colonies. He found that the regulations actually had little direct influence on the development of the American iron industry. No colonial iron works were reported to have been destroyed for disobeying the Parliamentary injunction against finishing mills. No colonist ever was prosecuted for evading or violating the restrictions. Perhaps if colonial fabricated iron products had sought a wider market, infringements would have been noticed and prosecuted. But the vast bulk of finished iron was used in the immediate vicinity of its production. Unless provincial governors were willing to actively seek out and destroy the illegal operations (and this they did not do), the Iron Act of 1750, like the Molasses Act of 1733, in actual practice was nullified. No matter how rigidly restrictive the statute reads in the law books, it appears to have had little or no direct effect on the development of the colonial iron industry.

Thus the three specific enactments of Parliament intended to protect British manufacturers from colonial competition—woolens, hats, and finished iron—appear to have been less than completely successful. Perhaps only in the case of hats was a potential American industry harmfully disrupted by legislation. But before concluding that the statutes were of only minor significance in shaping the colonial economy, it should be noted that there were also less direct, more subtle consequences of the British desire to regulate colonial competition. Lawrence A. Harper, for example, has discussed the possibility (it would be difficult to prove in any quantitative sense) that restrictive legislation, like the Iron Act, effectively discouraged investments of capital in the regulated industries, sending it to seek legal and presumably safer enterprises elsewhere. Curtis Nettels ("British Mercantilism and the Economic Development of the Thirteen Colonies," *The Journal of Economic History,* XII [Spring 1952]) has seen significance in other British regulations as they must have affected colonial industry. Britain regulated or proscribed colonial minting of currency, provincial corporations, commercial banks. The details of some of these policies will be discussed later, but it is useful to remember that these general regulations could touch the dimensions of economic opportunity within which the colonists lived.

Finally, in considering the application of industrial restraints upon the American provinces—the determined effort by Britain to shape the colonies in complementary rather than competitive forms—it is necessary to indicate that in areas other than direct competition, indeed in often only vaguely related endeavors, Britain's suspicious attitude about American industry generated regulation. Lawrence H. Gipson has shown one example which can demonstrate the point. In the first decade of the eighteenth century, the Virginians enacted a statute designed to encourage the development of towns in their province. Upon receipt of the law for review in England, suspicions were raised that, if allowed, it would tend to lessen tobacco production, which the Crown feared, since royal revenues would be affected, and also because the act might encourage manufacturing in Virginia. This was also a development Britain did not favor; the law was disallowed by King in Council. The direct consequences of industrial regulation may have had little to do with the actual shaping of the colonial economy, but the general British fears of a rising industrial America probably contributed indirectly to many aspects of imperial policy.

THE MONEY SUPPLY

In addition to Parliamentary legislation restricting ocean commerce, encouraging certain colonial pursuits, and regulating some competitive colonial industries, Britain also attempted to control American currency and coinage. Although this aspect of imperial regulation is sometimes ignored in general evaluations of British policy, such controls actually played immensely significant roles in shaping the patterns of American colonial life. Orthodox mercantilists insisted that the colonies be relegated to a properly dependent condition as far as the minting and circulation of coins were concerned; they viewed such restraints as necessary as regulation of commerce or industry. For gold and silver (specie, bullion) were the visible tokens of national wealth to mercantilists; the accumulation of such wealth in the homeland was a central tenet of their thought. As Britain defined the patterns of economic control within her Empire, increasingly restrictive measures shaped her imperial policy concerning coinage and currency.

The policy was built over a period of decades; the pattern of creation seems to have followed a rather consistent course of following each device the Americans initiated to overcome previous restrictions by new regulations to limit the new device. The theoretical objectives might be constant, but the methods adopted to gain those objectives shifted. First, in line with basic mercantilist belief, came a general proscription of the exportation of coins from the homeland to the colonies. While some parts of the Empire at times were released from this general rule (the trade to India, for example, required silver exports from Britain), the American colonies were never excepted from the restriction. This meant that English coins did not ordinarily circulate within the American dominions. Then a corollary was added, prohibiting the minting of coins in the provinces. No silver or gold mines had been discovered in British America, and there had been little effort to create a local coinage by operating colonial mints. Except for the brief experiment Massachusetts pursued with its "pine tree shillings," and a few other such endeavors, colonial mints had not matured. Now none ever would.

Denied the use of either the currency of the realm or of its own minting for the conduct of commerce and trade, the American colonists were forced to employ such expedient substitutes as they could arrange for themselves. They understood that neither their domestic, imperial, nor (when allowed) foreign commerce could fully develop without some medium of exchange. The southern plantation provinces relied upon credit arrangements with the British purchasers of their tobacco, rice, and indigo exports in the conduct of their trans-Atlantic trade. The system was unwieldy, placed the American producer in a poor bargaining position, and in time probably contributed to the historic indebtedness of the colonists—but it did work.

The problem faced by the northern colonists was, in comparison, more difficult. They had no staple export on which to build credits in Great Britain, so they were forced to concoct other devices. As indicated earlier, they had found their trade with the West Indies particularly useful, for from it they could carry away bills of credit on British merchants, or, even more desirable, specie in foreign coins. The Mediterranean markets of southern Europe were turned to the same employment. The specie or bills of credit obtained in the Indies or Mediterranean ports could be used for the purchase of British goods brought back to the northern provinces. Like the southern planters' credit arrangements, although roundabout and rife with hazards, the system worked. But the question to be asked, perhaps, is not whether it worked, but rather, how much more advantageous for the growth of the colonial economy alternate solutions might have proved. Had Britain ever relaxed her restrictions on coinage, or perhaps looked favorably upon the contemporary suggestions of a separate "imperial" coinage for trade purposes, a major handicap to colonial commerce would have been softened or removed.

Internally—that is, within the colonies—other devices were instituted as substitutes for coins. Besides barter and rudimentary credit arrangements of neighborhood variety, the American colonists constantly overvalued foreign coins in an endeavor to attract them to the mainland. Incidentally, Britain's sensitivity to this overvaluation of foreign coins, and her attempts to regulate the practice, indicate the significance of currency control to mercantile theorists. In the plantation provinces, which had created public warehousing for their staple crops, the colonists learned to use warehouse receipts as a local currency. And, in time, all of the mainland colonies experimented with paper money for domestic use. Colonial paper money was fiat money—notes issued by provincial governments, pledged to be redeemed by means of future tax revenues collected by the colony.

Beginning with a Massachusetts issue in 1690, the early emissions of paper currency were based on anticipated revenues, limited in duration to a few years' circulation, and were generally not made legal tender. Since the experiments worked quite satisfactorily for some of the colonies, by the end of Queen Anne's War (1713) there was a desire to continue the practice in peace-time. But the public emergency (defense, war) that had justified the issues was gone, and a new method of securing the bills seemed necessary. It was in answer to these conditions that the idea of creating "land banks" drew adherents.

A "land bank" was conceived on the basic premise of using a colony's most obvious resource—land—as security upon which paper money could be issued. The province would lend to land-holders its own fiat money. These loans would be retired in a stated number of years by the borrower, whose interest payments on the loan would provide income for operating the provincial government. The scheme promised advantages of circulating needed paper currency and of providing useful credit facilities for farmers, as well as public revenue. But the colonial merchants disliked the scheme, for it reduced their own economic power, in so far as they controlled local credit supplies. On occasion, as in South Carolina in the 1720's and especially in Massachusetts a little later, creditor merchants fought land-bank promoters in particularly impassioned contests. Parliament came to the aid of the beleaguered merchants in 1741, ending all land-bank promotions by extending the "Bubble Act" of 1720 (legislation which had outlawed unauthorized joint-stock companies in Britain) to the American dominions. And further restrictions on colonial currency experiments were forthcoming. In 1751 Parliament enacted a

Currency Act, again outlawing land banks and prohibiting the New England colonies from making bills of credit (paper money) legal tender.

Whatever may be said about imperial benefits and trans-Atlantic reciprocities in the general functioning of the Navigation Acts, Britain's monetary policies imposed upon the American provinces must be cited as one phase of imperial regulation which was narrowly conceived and proved a considerable handicap to the conduct of colonial enterprises, both at home and in overseas commerce. The policies instituted to regulate colonial currency, and the effects of those policies, consistently dramatized one of the basic assumptions of the Empire: the colonies were dependencies, and as such, on the especially sensitive questions of coinage and currency, their economic development was at best a secondary consideration, inferior in significance to the fundamental, primary objectives of British mercantilism. It would have been most surprising if it had been otherwise, yet it is necessary to keep this in mind in evaluating the economic empire. It is also necessary to remember that the colonists themselves were divided in their opinions about paper money and other methods of satisfying the needs created by the imperial restrictions.

A final facet of economic imperialism to be considered is the growth of the American colonies as markets for British goods. The population of the American mainland provinces increased from an estimated 75,000 in 1660 to 1,593,000 in 1760—a genuinely spectacular increase. As that population grew and extended its standard of living, the American market became correspondingly more significant, both in comparison with raw goods exported out of the colonies and in terms of the total trade of Great Britain. The use of the colonies as markets for British goods had been an admitted objective in mercantilist thought since before the first colony was planted in the New World. But, in their early years, with their small populations and limited purchasing power, the colonies' major attraction had been their value as sources of raw materials. By mid-eighteenth century the situation had changed, although it is doubtful if Britain fully considered that change in fixing imperial policies. George L. Beer would have argued that she did. He believed, for example, that the British decision, at the conclusion of the Great War for Empire, to retain Canada and restore to France the island of Guadalupe, was an indication of recognition in Britain of the changing nature of American trade, the increasing importance of the American market. But Clarence Ver Steeg, in *The Formative Years, 1607–1763*, argues otherwise, asserting that "contemporary letters, pamphlets, instructions, and legislation do not sustain this thesis."

To the extent that British imperial policies failed to recognize the growing importance of the colonies as markets and, instead, continued to concentrate on their attributes as producers of raw goods, imperial policy was out of step with the realities of the economic empire. Yet the general picture of imperial commerce as historians now paint it is a remarkably pleasant landscape. The estimates of the volume of that trade are revealing. Perhaps one-half of the total colonial trade was directly carried on with the mother country. It is estimated that in 1700 direct trade amounted to approximately one-sixth of the total trade of England; by 1770, the colonial trade had doubled its proportion and accounted for one-third of the total British trade. Obviously, such increases indicate vitality in the colonial economy and an increasingly significant role for those colonies in the economy of the British Empire.

AN ASSESSMENT

What then may be said in summary about the general effects of Britain's colonial system on the economy of the American colonies? In balance, it appears the Navigation Acts were not a major determinant, restricting the development of the provinces. Some significant sectors of the American economy, especially land-holding, were not directly regulated. Some specific enterprises—indigo, naval stores, shipbuilding—were enhanced by imperial encouragement. Other, and even larger, enterprises —tobacco and rice—developed within the machinery of imperial control and prospered from the central marketing features of the Empire. Some minor variants appear in the pattern;

the Hat Act, perhaps, and the Chesapeake fishing industry, which did not enjoy the privileges accorded to New England in importing foreign salt directly into America. But most historians consider the general effect of the legislation to have been more beneficial than burdensome to the colonies.

This general conclusion is derived not only from statistical evidence concerning the expansion of American commerce, industry, and agriculture. Other determining factors have been enlisted as evidence of the healthy state of the colonial economy. Professor Dickerson, for example, points to the rapid growth of population as one indicator of the vitality of the colonial economy. The population of British North America not only grew spectacularly; it increased at a much faster rate than did the British population. Some of this growth resulted from early marriages and large families (both useful as evidence of general well-being) and from the continuing, large immigration to the British colonies, an immigration which would never have taken place had the colonies not been economically attractive. The cultural institutions of colonial society—the churches, the colleges, the libraries, newspapers, and magazines—all indicate to Dickerson a thriving economy upon which colonists could base their social advances. American colonists were well-fed, well-housed, and enjoyed a considerable variety of the luxuries of life. In fact, in comparison with the Old World and with other parts of the New World, the British colonists enjoyed a high standard of living. They were able to accumulate goods and wealth, to import large numbers of Negro slaves and white servants. They filled up the tidewater and piedmont regions and, by the close of the colonial era, were ready to spill westward over the mountains. Such were the colonial benefits, says Dickerson, of the Empire.

Not all scholars, it is true, are as enthusiastic about the imperial pattern as Dickerson is; many are more willing than he to spot flaws in the structure and to emphasize specific features of regulation which worked to the colonists' disadvantage. They would temper the glow of enthusiasm by indicating the sometimes narrow, limited view of imperial planners. They would place more emphasis upon genuinely burdensome features of imperial regulation, such as the controls on currency and even upon ineffective yet discriminatory restraints like the Molasses Act. But even with such modifications, the general conclusion stands, for it does appear that those parts of the imperial system which, in theory, would have been most unfortunately oppressive to the colonists were mitigated by geography, the relegation of colonial problems to a subordinate position among British affairs of state, or bureaucratic inefficiency. This allowed enough room for colonial expansion to keep American unhappiness at a relatively low level.

What happened to the economic empire after 1763 is not within the province of this essay. But by that date it was obvious that a relatively mature and profitable economy had developed in the British colonies. And, having tasted the fruits of such a system, the Americans could be expected to defend their standard of living against all threats—real and imaginary—and to work to increase even further the promises of American colonial life.

THREE

Imperial Politics and Warfare

Economic considerations were primarily responsible for the creation of the first British Empire, and throughout its existence theories and plans for economic gain remained matters of great sensitivity among British imperialists. In time, European wars involving other nations with their own American empires and interests brought Britain's colonial areas into strategic considerations, often dramatically straining relationships between parent state and the American dominions. Then there was a less sensitive, less dramatic sphere of imperial concern—the more routine, day-to-day political arrangements through which Britain attempted to direct her colonies toward her economic and strategic goals. Upon the contours of the constitutional structure by which Britain governed her overseas Empire, and the responsiveness or lack of responsiveness of the colonists to imperial direction, much of the economic and strategic benefit of the Empire would depend. Within the colonies, those same constitutional connections, in varying degrees, helped to shape the structure of American politics and society.

If there was division between theory and practice in the economic features of the British Empire, something of the same division also existed in the constitutional-political imperial affairs. In theory the Empire was, or should be, a relatively tidy unit, with a structure capable of analysis and examination, perhaps even to the point of creating tables of organization and charts of command. In actuality, the first British Empire, in its administrative features, lacked clarity and precision. Several major elements contributed to this. Historically, the colonies were created before the Empire, and partly through design, probably through desire, Britain never established rigid, central controls over her dominions similar to those of Spain and France. During the seventeenth century, and to a lesser extent the years following, the homeland was engaged in re-shaping its own constitutional structure, and this contributed to the ill-defined nature of imperial relationships. These circumstances contributed, among other things, to the diffusion of responsibility for imperial affairs through a great variety of agencies and bureaus of state. Finally, as in the economic aspects of imperial control, local, colonial realities often frustrated Britain's policies.

The supremacy of Parliamentary authority was a central tenet of the British constitution as defined by the Whig settlement after the Glorious Revolution. Ineffectual efforts by small groups during the eighteenth century to return to Stuart rule only emphasized the basic commitment to legislative supremacy. Parliament's primary position encompassed not only affairs at home; the constitution extended beyond the shores of Britain to the dominions. Throughout the colonial era, until the crises preceding the American Revolution brought forth contrary interpretations from the colonists, there is little evidence to indicate colonial opposition to the "settlement." Americans not only understood it, they supported it. Lawrence H. Gipson has demonstrated that not only did Parliament act in accordance with the theory in its enactment of trade regulations, currency laws, statutes regarding aliens, and other matters; the colonists themselves acknowledged Parliamentary authority. For example, in 1754, in their efforts to re-define colonial-imperial relationships through the Albany Plan of Union, the Americans believed Parliamentary approval would be necessary to implement the plan. Yet over and against this theory and practice of Parliamentary supremacy stood the earlier theory and time-honored traditions of Crown responsibility for imperial affairs. Parliament not only seemed at times reluctant to originate measures to bring order in the Empire by enacting statutes creating common patterns of colonial government; it generally contented itself with allowing routine affairs of the Empire to be handled by administrative commissions and boards.

Exactly how those commissions and boards of imperial control governed the Empire in the eighteenth century has been exhaustively studied and described by scholars. Charles M. Andrews devoted the fourth volume of his monumental *The Colonial Period of American History* to the topic; his contemporary in exploring American origins within the British Empire, Herbert L. Osgood, added other dimensions in his multi-volume *The American Colonies in the Eighteenth Century* (1924). And the first half of the twentieth century saw the production of a great quantity of specialized studies which described, analyzed, and explained the British instruments of imperial control. Many of them came from the graduate students of Andrews and Osgood. While there remain fruitful areas for historical research, as Dora M. Clark's *The Rise of the British Treasury* (1960) and Thomas Barrow's *Trade and Empire: The British Customs Service in Colonial America* indicate, by and large, the details of imperial administration have been set forth.

From these imperial studies, the agencies of administration may be studied. Besides the Parliament of Great Britain, along with the slowly evolving cabinet system of ministries, the state offices and agencies sharing responsibility for colonial affairs included the Privy Council, the Board of Trade, the Secretary of State for the Southern Department (who exercised the patronage for the colonies except during intervals when the president of the Board of Trade claimed it), the Treasury Board, the Commissioners of the Customs, the Admiralty, War, and Audit offices. Ecclesiastical matters concerning the Anglican Church in America fell within the jurisdiction of the Bishop of London. From the provinces, but resident in Britain, came the agents of the individual colonies, delegates from the dominions to dispense requested information about their provinces and to "represent" provincial interests. These were the instruments of empire in Britain. Obviously, in the decades stretching from the Glorious Revolution to the American Revolution, such a diffusion of responsibility for colonial affairs provided room for a host of statesmen, politicians, clerks, and placemen to test their theories and exercise their authority. The surprising part of it all, in many ways, is the fact that there was so little, not so much experimentation; that basic patterns remained so little changed, not so often altered.

Of course there was some shifting in objectives and procedures. Imperial administration reflected changes in the governing practices within Great Britain itself, the coming and going of personnel, economic expansion, population changes, shifts in social theories and pressures. Diplomacy and war brought differing emphases in imperial affairs. But, in overview, these alterations appear less significant than the adherence with which Britain followed the basic theories laid down during the last decades of the seventeenth century, particularly as they were "formalized" in the decisions of William III after the Glorious Revolution. Those decisions reflected the general theories of imperial administration and, as a result, the presumed nature of American colonial government. The decision to restore the colonies to their status as of around 1670 ensured a continuation of the mixed system which had developed to that time, with some provinces directly regulated by the Crown, others retained by or restored to their proprietors, and, in the case of Rhode Island, Connecticut, and (in modified form) Massachusetts, re-establishment of their chartered privileges.

Within this mixture of forms, however, a dominant "type" emerged; the "typical" American province in the eighteenth century was a royal colony. If Britain did not achieve her never-completely-forgotten goal of eventual reduction of all colonies to this form, at least the majority of the American provinces were so shaped. New Hampshire was returned to that status after the collapse of the Dominion of New England; Massachusetts, partially by terms of her charter of 1691; New York; New Jersey after the surrender of governing rights by the proprietors in 1702; Maryland, until the Calverts regained their political rights in 1715; Virginia; the two Carolinas after the purchase of the proprietary in 1729; Georgia, with the surrender of its charter by the trustees in 1752; the West India island possessions since the post-Restoration years; and, to the north, Newfoundland and Nova Scotia, added in the eighteenth century. These were the royal provinces—the "typical" British-American colonies of the old Empire.

THE ROYAL GOVERNOR

In the royal provinces, the character, ability, and personality of the Crown-appointed governor theoretically was of great significance in shaping the political, economic, and social life of the colony. While we lack a modern, general evaluation of the royal governors, several recent studies have delineated the careers of individual governors or, in a less direct fashion, by analyzing provincial politics have broadened our understanding of the governors' role. John Schutz, in *William Shirley: King's Governor of Massachusetts* (1961), William Abbot, in his study of *The Royal Governors of Georgia, 1774–1775* (1959), and Lawrence Leder, in *Robert Livingston and the Politics of Colonial New York, 1664–1728* (to mention only three of many such studies), have considerably amplified our knowledge of the royal governors in America and the part they played in the day-to-day operations of the Empire.

Leder, in his study of Livingston's New York career, for example, emphasizes the contributions that Robert Hunter, an able royal governor, made toward creation of long-delayed political stability in that province. Abbot credits Georgia's more astute governors with major contributions to that frontier province's advances. Possessed of considerable potential authority, the governor's office could be and often was used in a constructive way to determine the direction of colonial development. The governor was the central force of imperial authority within his province; whatever actual success British designs might have necessarily rested upon the royal governors' understanding, and their willingness and ability to direct their colonies toward those imperial objectives.

As the primary British officer in a royal province, the governor was the natural center of imperial officialdom, around whom other imperial agents—customs officers, naval officers, surveyors general, attorneys general, receivers general, and others—gravitated. Some sought his advice, some his favor. He was expected to give encouragement and direction and might, without great effort, find himself the leader of what some historians have termed the "court party" or "court faction" in provincial politics. His fellow agents in imperial management were naturally attached to his group. Colonists who sought his favors and preferments might also join.

The interests of provincials could coincide with the governor's interests, for his powers extended beyond the duties of administering imperial statutes and orders within his assigned province. As governor, by his commission and instructions, he possessed authority bearing directly on the course of provincial political events. He nominated men to the Council, the group of royally appointed advisers who, in conjunction with the governor, administered colonial affairs, formed the upper house of the colonial legislature, and sat in judicial capacity as the highest court in most of the provinces. In his joint activities with the Council, the governor could direct the course of legislation, land distribution, defense measures, and justice. His powers (at least theoretically) over the elected lower house of assembly, and through that agency into the domestic political life of the province, were also ample. He held an absolute veto over legislation, and the power to summon, adjourn, prorogue, and dissolve the assembly. And, if astute, he could extend his authority into the realm of local government, the county and sub-county levels where his powers of appointment could be used to reward friends and punish opponents, thereby advancing his designs for the province or his own career.

Thus the governor was, or might become, the central agent both in imperial affairs and in domestic activities within his province. If he was a man of limited ability, with narrowly conceived ambitions or views of his province's needs, he might be unable to control factionalism and political strife, and the province and his own reputation became the poorer. Lawrence Leder has shown the results of a series of such New York governors. On the other hand, an able, determined governor like Robert Hunter of New York, as described by Leder, or Governors Ellis and Wright of Georgia, as seen by Abbot, or Massachusetts Governor Shirley, as portrayed by John Schutz, could advance both the province's and his own interests, stabilizing political activities, working diligently to accentuate programs of compatible interest to colony and Empire, and effectively reducing the areas of contention between home and America.

In many respects the governor's life was not enviable. His position tended to make him like the proverbial servant with two masters, capable of satisfying neither. Not only did he need to build a position of strength domestically within the province and to identify himself as being at least concerned about, if not always wholly committed to local ambitions and aspirations; he was dependent for continued tenure in office upon men and interests in the homeland which often—perhaps usually—bore little relationship to or interest in imperial designs. In the flexible, shifting political world of eighteenth-century Britain, a governor achieved office because of his relationships to those in power, not because of his administrative abilities; his continuation in office depended upon his talents in retaining a base of support back home.

Despite this, he needed also to consider the institutions and directions he received from the official agencies in England charged with administration of colonial affairs—the Board of Trade, the Treasury, the Customs Commissioners, and all of the other agencies involved. Beset, then, with both theoretical objectives and practical considerations on both sides of the Atlantic, the governor was unlikely to satisfy all the demands upon him. Perhaps the significant conclusion from a survey of the careers of those men who held the office during the eighteenth century is not their failures to advance imperial designs, but rather their ability to accommodate, to the extent that they did, the imperial needs with the local interests and desires.

If, until after 1763, the American colonists entertained no serious thoughts about "independence" or life outside the imperial orbit—and historians seem agreed that this was true—then the royal governors, the central agents bridging Britain and her colonies, did prove sufficiently flexible, useful agents in accommodating differences, allowing scope for satisfactory expression of both imperial and colonial aspirations. How much "accident" and how much "design" were involved in this situation is difficult to determine. As indicated earlier, Britain never proceeded in her imperial plans from assumptions of control structured along such rigid lines as Spanish or French imperial regimentation. British colonial governors were expected to dominate and direct colonial administration, but not to monopolize it. Yet even with these moderate "theoretical" powers assigned to the governors, it was probably more accident than design that led to the erosion of authority from the office, providing increasing opportunities for colonial participation in government. Distance from the seat of Empire, and the slowness of eighteenth-century communication, contributed to the separation between the theory and the practice. So did the diffusion of responsibility for colonial affairs among the various agencies within the British government. It is a fact that, until very late in the colonial era, no royal governor was removed from his office directly because he disobeyed his instructions. Warfare with France and Spain, and its attendant crises in America, created moments of emergency when rules could be ignored for immediate needs, thus setting precedents and procedures which were continued in years of peace. The results of all this can be seen in the American attitudes toward royal governors. Some were loved, a few were detested, but the office was rarely damned as an engine of perpetual tyranny. The longer the colonists lived with the system, the more they learned to work its weaknesses into their advantages.

It is significant, but often forgotten when viewing colonial America only through the window of the American Revolution, that in Pennsylvania and Maryland (two remaining proprietary provinces) colonists exerted considerable effort to cast off proprietary rule and to substitute royal status in its place. The Americans working for that change obviously assumed that a royally appointed governor would prove a more acceptable executive than a governor representing a proprietor; that more local autonomy was possible in a province tied directly to the Crown than in a colony held by Calverts or Penns.

From a twentieth-century "managerial" viewpoint, with its emphasis on efficient administration, eighteenth-century royal governorships left much to be desired. At any given moment, chaotic conditions would seem to have been the rule. But, in the larger sense of historical development, the royal governors evidently served as useful "shock absorbers," softening and cushioning collisions between local and imperial ambitions. That cushioning effect, however, played to the ultimate advantage of the colonies, for they gradually assumed ever greater controls over their own development. In filling the vacuums of power as they discovered them during the course of the years to 1763, they built precedents and established procedures of local control that one day would prove disastrous for the Empire.

THE LOWER HOUSES OF ASSEMBLY

The theory of the Empire fixed the royal governor as the central agency of colonial government. In actual practice, however, by the close of the colonial era the elected lower houses of assembly had come to more than a position of parity in power with the governors—they had eclipsed them as the principal instruments of governmental power within the provinces. The rise of the colonial assemblies and the contests for power they waged with royal governors to achieve political authority have long been staple ingredients in the historian's narrative of colonial development. New details of that story have lately been explained, for the southern provinces, in Jack P. Greene's study of the lower houses of assembly, *The Quest for Power* (1963). While the corresponding history of the lower houses in the middle and northern provinces needs similar study, there is probably much in Greene's findings that is applicable throughout the American colonial experience.

The story, again, is the story of division between theory and practice, between the ideal of Empire as envisioned by British theorists on the one hand and the actual functioning government in America on the other. It constitutes as significant a pattern in the history of political development as in the economic history of the Empire. Theory and ideals pointed toward a unified, consolidated imperial structure, with Crown, Parliament, and colonial administrators linked in logical arrangements for governing the overseas dominions. Over and against the theory was the actual developing practice of government in the colonies, affording opportunities for the lower houses of assembly, elected by and responsive to the wishes of the colonists themselves, to reach out and attain ever greater measures of control.

Historians have long pointed to the control of colonial revenues as the primary mechanism by which the lower houses of assembly gained power at the expense of royal governors. The "power of the purse" has been pictured as the weapon of control in the colonies, in rough similarity to Parliament's financial regulation of the declining royal power at home. The governors, caught between colonial and imperial forces, were brought to surrender by the Americans' insistence on their right to regulate public finances, including the sensitive matter of the governors' own salaries. Greene, however, has shown that this simplified explanation of the shifting center of governing control is too rudimentary to describe satisfactorily the actual situation in the southern provinces. He demonstrates, in fact, both the complexities of the shift, which extended into a vast number of areas and concerns, and the fact that the governors' salaries, far from being the only, or even the major, method of gaining ascendancy over the royal executives, was not a major controversy in the southern provinces. For there, in most cases, the governors were provided with annual salaries from sources beyond the reach of the local assemblies.

The development of legislative control, according to Greene, was a much more complex story, developing along a variety of "fronts" and bringing a mixture of successes and failures to the colonists as they pursued the quest for power for their lower houses of assembly. Public finance was one of the major areas in which the lower houses satisfied that quest, but in a more extensive manner than merely manipulating governors' salaries. The southern provinces used the power to tax as a springboard from which they eventually gathered the right to frame general supervisory control over finances of a public nature, including the right to audit accounts of public officers, appoint and maintain public treasurers, order the dispersal of public funds, and (although circumscribed by the imperial restrictions) engage in emission of paper money. And, while the governors' salaries were not within the regulating range of the lower houses, the fees and thus the fortunes accruing to the executives were, and the control of fees, added to the increasing list of other methods of regulating financial affairs, gave to the lower houses of assembly the primary position in colonial money matters. This position, once gained, could be used as a lever for securing authority in other governmental concerns.

Control of raising and dispersing public moneys, for example, could be used as an instrument for exercising control over public services, such as public printing, with its corresponding regulatory authority over public information; the agency, or "representation" of colonial affairs in London; military matters, Indian affairs, judicial concerns, and even ecclesiastical affairs. The penetration of assembly influence into all of these varied areas of government certainly was not uniformly successful, nor did it occur simultaneously in all of the southern provinces. But what Greene has discerned as immensely significant is that, in their quest for power, all of the lower houses of assembly in the plantation provinces moved to establish themselves as a part of the decision-making, policy-setting machinery in all of these areas. And all of the southern houses had achieved some measure of success in their quest by 1763.

There were directions where the drive for legislative power made only short or no headway, and even directions where power once exercised by colonial assemblymen was regained by imperial authorities. Greene identifies the movement to control the "composition and proceedings" of the lower houses themselves as one segment of the contest in which some of the most significant colonial aspirations were never realized. The model used by the colonial assemblies in their quest was the pattern of the House of Commons of Great Britain. The American colonists consciously viewed their local assemblies as miniature replicas of the Commons; they sought duplication of privileges and immunities enjoyed by members of Parliament for their local legislators. In some areas they succeeded, winning recognition of members' freedom in speech, in debate, and from arrest, as well as the right to settle disputed elections and to choose the speaker of the lower house. But on other, quite significant matters their drive was frustrated. They never completely gained their desired control of scheduling elections or sessions. Representation, or apportionment, was controlled through the device of creating new counties, often by dividing established counties. In these matters the colonists made little or no headway against the Crown's determination to retain control.

But, in Greene's view, these failures or setbacks were of less significance than the gains the colonists made. If they did not achieve absolute victory in their quest for power, they did succeed in effecting sufficient changes to alter the basic constitutional arrangements of the Empire. By 1763, the center of power in the colonies was no longer to be found in the royal governor and his agencies of control, but rather in the lower houses of assembly. And herein was a real division between theory and practice. For the Americans were living within an imperial structure operating in a fashion quite different from the structure Britain believed to be outlined by her constitutional arrangements bridging homeland and provinces. "From Edward Randolph in the last decades of the seventeenth century to the . . . 1750s," Greene concludes, "colonial officials had envisoned a highly centralized empire with a uniform political system in each of the colonies and with the imperial government closely supervising the subordinate governments. But because they had never made any sustained or systematic attempt to achieve these goals during the first half of the eighteenth century, there had developed a working arrangement permitting the lower houses considerable latitude in shaping colonial constitutions without requiring Crown or Proprietary officials to give up any of their ideals. That there had been a growing divergence between imperial theory and colonial practice mattered little so long as each refrained from openly challenging the other." One day, of course, the challenges would come, but that day was still in the future.

COLONISTS AND GOVERNMENT

There was another level of government in the British American colonies, below the imperial agencies and the provincial institutions, which perhaps most directly affected the average colonist. The ordinary citizen, concerned with the daily routine of getting and spending—sheltering and feeding and defending himself and his family—probably was aware of imperial actions, or even colonial legislators, only during unusual, perhaps only emergency moments. Such a colonist dealt most directly with his county or town government, which had been developed in answer to the needs of the local communities. These local—county or town—governments have been termed the most stable agencies of government in colonial America. Wesley F. Craven, in his study of *The Southern Colonies in the Seventeenth Century,* has pointed to the need for more fully appreciating the role local governments played in colonial development; Clarence Ver Steeg, in *The Formative Years, 1607–1763,* endorses the theme: "Rebellions might come and go, but local government provided an anchor that enabled the colonials to weather the storm. Indeed, the fact that local government in

America has survived a revolution, a civil war, an industrial revolution, and global responsibilities is one of the most impressive yet most neglected aspects in the history of American political institutions." Ver Steeg suggests that, in addition to their vitality and usefulness, the local governments also provided a basically divisive force within the colonial world. In England, local government was administered directly through agencies related to the national government and thus furnished a vehicle for furthering a "vertical-type" nationalism. Conversely, in the colonies, local government tended to operate in a manner which discouraged centralization and uniformity.

It is, perhaps, easier to see this result in the New England region than in the southern provinces. The New England town meetings afforded convenient and presumably democratic methods for conducting local public affairs. The freemen of a town could participate directly in fashioning policies for the community, generally divorced from influence or pressures from provincial or imperial interests. In the southern provinces, county governments were the primary agencies of local administration and there imperial influences theoretically might be exerted through the royal governor's appointive power in the offices of the justice of the peace. The justices were the chief local administrators, combining supervision of local public affairs with their judicial duties. Since they were appointed by the governor, rather than elected, and since they might also be in the governor's debt for commissions as local militia officers or other favors, they were theoretically less free as agents than the town officers in New England. Yet, in many cases, the governor's theoretical powers had been closely circumscribed by methods of nomination, and in the southern as well as the northern colonies, local administrators exercised their powers relatively free from imperial regulation.

Their duties were such that their offices rarely became arenas of contest between local and imperial interests; their function, and their virtue, resulted from their generally uninterrupted attention to the routine needs of their immediate communities. Whether northern or southern, town or county, the officers of local administration supervised the construction, maintenance, and operation of roads, bridges, and ferries. They looked after welfare needs of orphans, widows, and indigents. They organized and supplied militia units. They worried about broken fences and stray cattle. They set tax levies and collected revenue, licensed grog houses and taverns, and dispensed justice in minor litigation. The ordinary settler paid his taxes to this government, looked to it for protection, and resorted to its courts when he sought justice. By its stability in times of crisis, its familiarity as a permanent fixture of his immediate world—like the church, chapel, or burying ground—it represented law, order, and authority in the settler's known world of his own community. Provincial government and provincial politics were removed and distant, perhaps several days' travel away. As for imperial administration and the affairs of the Empire, they were even more remote and of less concern.

This "layered" arrangement—extending from the British Crown and Parliament through royal officials resident in the colonies, to colonial assemblies and down to the local units of administration, town and county governments—provided the framework within which colonial political life operated. It was always, everywhere, a highly mixed and richly varied structure. Within it could be found places of honor and places of fortune; offices appointive and offices elective; elements of aristocracy and elements of democracy. Lacking precision and uniformity, it seems almost to defy general description. Yet historians continue to ask the question, and to seek its answer: What was the nature of the political life, and the society shaping and shaped by the politics of provincial America? Was the over-all tone of colonial life aristocratic, structured by institutions and inclinations into stratified classes assuring political, social, and economic privileges to the few? Or was colonial life democratic, exhibiting unusual (for its, or perhaps any, age) opportunities for individual satisfaction in political, social, and economic aspirations?

These questions have engendered more debate in recent years than almost any other interpretive problem concerning colonial America. Much of the interest in the questions has originated in attempts to assess the nature of the American Revolution, which have led, in turn, to analyses of the structure of pre-Revolutionary provincial politics and society. The "case" for a democratic interpretation of colonial life, with particular emphasis on political democracy, has been argued by Robert E. Brown in *Middle-Class Democracy and the Revolution in Massachusetts, 1691–1780* (1955), and in a second study, written in co-authorship with his wife, B. Katherine Brown, *Virginia, 1705–1786: Democracy or Aristocracy?* (1964). In seeking answers to the question, the Browns have relied upon two major types of evidence—statistical analyses of voting records and population characteristics, and indications of contemporary opinions regarding the nature of political and social structures from the literary remains of the eighteenth century. The conclusions they reach from their evidence are generally unqualified assertions of provincial democracy in both Massachusetts and Virginia.

The statistical analyses of suffrage in the colonies presented in these studies seems more convincing than the expressions of contemporary opinion concerning democratic or aristocratic tendencies. The Massachusetts characterizations, in particular, too often are drawn from statements of British officials attempting to explain failure or frustration of their administration on the basis of "excessive" colonial democracy. Although some critics have questioned the statistical methods employed, historians generally have been more interested in, and probably more persuaded by, the Browns' assertions concerning voting privileges and restrictions. They have found that the suffrage regulations laid down for the electorate of members of the lower houses of assembly were much less restrictive than formerly had been supposed. In both Massachusetts and Virginia, the property qualifications were easily met by the majority of adult white male colonists. The Browns emphasize who could vote, not who did vote, for it appears that the suffrage, although widely distributed among the Virginia and Massachusetts colonists, was less widely exercised.

These assertions of colonial American democracy have converted some scholars, but not all, and the controversy continues. Critics of this basically unqualified characterization of provincial politics as "democratic" have raised some valid queries. Merrill Jensen, for example, in "Democracy and the American Revolution," *Huntington Library Quarterly,* XX (August 1957), asserts that ". . . colonial governments on the eve of the Revolution did not function democratically, nor did the men who controlled them believe in democracy. Even if we agree that there was virtually manhood suffrage, in Massachusetts, it is difficult . . . to see it as a democracy. In 1760 the government was controlled by a superb political machine headed by Thomas Hutchinson, who with his relatives and political allies occupied nearly every important political office in the colony except the governorship. The Hutchinson oligarchy controlled the superior court, the council, the county courts, and the justices of the peace; with this structure of appointive office spread throughout the colony, it was able to control the house of representatives elected by the towns . . . if Massachusetts had a democratic leader, that man was Thomas Hutchinson, a charge to which he would have been the first to issue a horrified denial."

As for the governorship, which Hutchinson did not control, that office was filled by Crown appointment. And in Virginia, an even larger proportion of provincial officers were appointed, not elected. The Browns, in their study of Virginia, seem to concede something of the argument in a brief but significant section of their analysis, indicating that the colonial voters there enjoyed a direct voice only in the selection of members of the House of Burgesses. All other Virginia offices were filled by appointment. The conditions and procedures by which candidates announced or were chosen for office also needs more study. How fully were all interests in colonial society represented in the slates of candidates? What barriers, if any, disqualified some men from consideration and what encouragements, if any, propelled others toward public service?

Interesting and debate-inspiring though the question of democracy, or its limitations, in colonial America is, it need not have concerned us in this general review of colonial-imperial relationships except for one fact: The Browns have interpreted American opposition to British imperial regulations largely in terms of a dichotomy between aristocracy and democracy. The British Empire, or at least its agents, in their view, was aristocratic; the American colonies were democratic. As Robert Brown has stated it in a review, colonial democracy and British imperialism were "two essentially incompatible forces"; it was democracy in the colonies which kept the mercantile system from being effectively enforced and threatened independence from imperial rule. In *Middle-Class Democracy and the Revolution in Massachusetts,* Brown explains that ". . . in all this, there was no hint of a controlling aristocracy . . . opposed to a disfranchised and under-privileged class; in fact, the British would have been much happier than they were if such an aristocracy existed. What was needed was some way to curtail the over-abundance of democratic customs which already existed, so that Britain could enforce her mercantile system and secure the dependence of the colonies on the mother country."

This reading of the history of imperial relationships tends to polarize imperial-provincial interests, connoting monomorphic political and social conditions in the colonies and in imperial agencies. It leaves little room for the more subtle identification of interest groupings which other historians have described as characteristic of provincial society—groups which, in the fluidity of colonial social structures, ordinarily divided between an older, more mature elite, enjoying social, economic, and political power, and a newer, rising group, perhaps already in possession of economic power and anxious to gain corresponding social and political privileges. In the Browns' view, there was no real American aristocracy; in the opposing view, there were both aristocrats and would-be aristocrats, either or both willing to align themselves with or against imperial agencies according to their estimates of how such alignment might help or hinder their own welfare. In one view, the friction was always between colonists and Empire; in the other, friction could be generated as easily by internal struggles as by imperial relationships. In fact, as long as colonial opportunities for individual advancement existed and colonial society remained fluid, such frictions were very likely to develop.

A further difference in interpretation results from the

assertion by Robert Brown that the frictions between the democratic colonies and the aristocratic Empire were constant features of imperial politics. He has labeled the state of the Empire one of "perpetual discordance," filled with inevitable clashes between the democratic, colonial way of life and an aristocratic British philosophy. Other scholars, impressed with the beneficial effects of imperial relationships, have characterized the normal state of the Empire as harmonious, with the occasional eruption of discordance the exception, not the rule. Between these two characterizations—discordance and harmony—there seems little room for a composite assessment.

Whatever the "normal" state of imperial relationships (and no final statement would satisfy all historians), international warfare and its accompanying dislocations brought crises in understanding between parent state and provinces. Imperial defense and aggressive warfare against neighboring empires placed unusual strains upon British-colonial relationships, exposing otherwise half-hidden cleavages between them.

THE EMPIRE IN WAR

The basic motivation for forging an English Empire in the years from 1660 to 1690 had been economic in nature. American colonies, regulated in England's interest, would magnificently increase the trade of English merchants, generate revenues for the Crown, and hopefully bring profits from land-holding to proprietary lords and gentlemen. These economic considerations, and the endeavors to fashion an imperial system to further them, led in a direct line to policies establishing political controls and clarifying constitutional relationships between colonies and mother country. After 1689, while economic impulses would continue to exert significant influences in imperial statecraft, the basic motivating forces propelling most of the attempts to unify and strengthen imperial controls probably stemmed from strategic and military considerations. Beginning in 1689 with the War of the League of Augsburg (King William's War, in America), Britain would wage a long and costly series of conflicts against France and her allies—the War of the Spanish

Succession (Queen Anne's War), the War of Jenkin's Ear against Spain, which merged into the more comprehensive War of the Austrian Succession (King George's War), and the final conflict, the Great War for Empire (French and Indian War, Seven Years' War), ending in 1763. Each of these conflicts precipitated occasions for Britain to consider her American provinces in a manner different from older, earlier concepts.

Theoretical strategic arguments for creation and maintenance of an overseas Empire had been part of the rationale for imperial endeavors from the beginning. But not until after 1689 were such theories actually put to major tests. Then the potential strategic and military advantages and disadvantages of overseas possessions became sensitive considerations in shaping policies for the Empire. Klaus Knorr, in his analysis of *British Colonial Theories, 1570–1850* (1944), identified four separate arguments stressing strategic advantages which British theorists and publicists claimed would accrue from possession of overseas territories. Each of them contributed in some measure to the over-all impulse for Empire building.

The first assertion stressed the advantage which overseas colonies would bring to Britain in any endeavor she might make to attack the colonies of enemy nations or harass the trade of enemy empires. During the sixteenth and early seventeenth centuries, such thought presumably was directed against Spanish enterprises: British colonies in America would offer convenient bases for hostile raids on Spanish possessions and commerce. Secondly, in a more general fashion, overseas colonies would bring Britain increased mastery of the seas. A third advantage the imperialists predicted from an overseas empire was the function such colonies might play in the homeland's constant concern to maintain security through a "balance of power" among European nations, some of which were also building non-European empires. If other powers—Spain, France, Holland—became threateningly overweighted because of their Asian, African, or American colonies, Britain would need colonies of her own to restore an equilibrium. Finally, arguing a defensive role for overseas possessions, it was suggested that the

time might well come when new or expanded colonial possessions might be required to safeguard and protect valuable
British colonies already in existence. This last function assumed
a continuing commitment in Empire building; in contests for
empire, the homeland might be forced to establish defensive
colonies to protect mature possessions from hostile rivals.

Thus, at least in theory, colonies were strategically, mili-
tarily useful to the mother country, capable of offering both defensive and offensive benefits in the nation's trade rivalries,
diplomacy, and warfare against enemy states. In the eighteenth
century the British people would be given an opportunity to
test these theories from an earlier era and to discover that,
along with the strategic benefits colonies offered, there was also
a price to be paid. The "price of Empire" turned out to be the
cost of defending it, for an increasingly large expenditure
in men and money was required to safeguard British dominions
already established. Ultimately even the last of the early theories proved true, for European powers eventually sought to
balance their world by waging warfare in America.

There had been a time in the earlier years of European
expansion and colony building when the overseas possessions
had been considered a separate sphere, divorced from the
wars of European statecraft. The concept of there being
"no peace beyond the line" of demarcation had created two
worlds, and the American world was not part of the European
world as far as conventional diplomacy and warfare were concerned. What this meant was that Europeans could raid, plun-
der, and even capture New World settlements of other nations
without such activities interfering with the regular relationships between those powers in Europe.

Perhaps partly because the rules of the game separated warfare in Old and New worlds, and perhaps also because it coincided with the basic royal policy of extending no direct financial
subsidy for discovery or colonization, the English theory of
imperial defense was rooted in the basic belief that the American colonists could, would, and should protect themselves. This
is the view of John Shy, who has reviewed that theory in the introductory chapter of *Toward Lexington: The Role of the*

British Army in the Coming of the American Revolution (1965). But having set down the theory under which imperial defense was structured—basic dependence upon colonial militia units, locally raised, equipped, and officered—Shy hastens to fill out the story by demonstrating that the theory, like so many imperial theories, often was ignored in the exigencies of the actual occasion. Britain did commit military forces and naval power to the defense of the American Empire. Fictitious though the theory may have become, it was not renounced until 1754 when, after a century and a half of allegiance to the older view, Britain reversed her assumptions to square more closely with the realities of the Empire. Then, at the start of the Great War for Empire, Britain decided to commit men and money in major proportions in order to defeat France, not in Europe, but in America. The alternative would have been to allow France to win the Ohio Valley, something neither the British nor the American colonists desired.

In the evolving partnership in warfare which linked Britain and her American colonies in changing circumstances during the years from 1689 to 1763, there was ample time for ideas and concepts to grow or to be modified. Lessons learned in the early conflicts might be remembered during later events, and ideas dimly perceived at the beginning of the eighteenth century might well have become strong convictions by 1755. The military partnership almost inevitably generated misunderstandings and grievances that marred imperial harmony. If, given the modern instruments for communication and control that twentieth-century military men are able to command, partners in alliances still argue about goals and procedures, how much more reasonable to expect that British imperial relationships would have felt strains and tuggings during attempts at co-operatively waging war.

Even an unadorned list of imperial misunderstandings, jealousies, quarrels, and grievances would fill the pages of a book; a few examples must suffice to illustrate the nature of the problems. During Queen Anne's War, in 1709, after plans had been laid for a joint assault upon French Canada, Britain decided not to commit the force she had agreed to furnish for the operation and delayed for several months notifying the colonists of her decision. George M. Waller, in his biography *Samuel Vetch: Colonial Enterpriser* (1960), comments that "it was only good sense" for the ministry in England to defer British forces from joining the Americans, since peace-making then was going in Europe and it appeared that captured colonies would be restored to their previous owners if the negotiations were successful. But, Waller adds, while this exonerates the British in the basic decision, at the time the reasons for the abrupt change were not known to the Americans, and thus were of no aid in alleviating their unhappiness. What made the situation even worse was that the colonists, for once, had really exerted themselves to prepare their part for the combined attack. And the cavalier attitude of the British, in their failure to inform the Americans of their decision in time to halt preparations in the colonies, indicated a lack of consideration which could only aggrieve the colonists who were trying to co-operate in a venture of common interest.

Trevor R. Reese, in *Colonial Georgia: A Study of British Imperial Policy in the Eighteenth Century* (1963), similarly assesses an incident of 1740, when a planned attack on St. Augustine in Spanish Florida failed because of insufficient support from Britain. Reese shows that however significant the capture of the place might have appeared to the Georgians, in the larger strategy of the war a minor objective like St. Augustine could not and should not have been allowed to divert energies or attention from more significant objectives on the Continent or elsewhere in the Western Hemisphere. And similar episodes could be repeated over and over again. The return to France of the fortress at Louisbourg on Cape Breton Island, captured by the Americans during King George's War and returned to France as part of the peace settlement ending that war, insulted the colonists' pride. Nor were strategic planning, poor communications, inefficient procedures, or indifferent attitudes the only causes for American bitterness toward mother Britain in war-time. Matters of military rank between colonial units and regular British army forces, the quotas requested in men and supplies, impressment or attempts at impressment of colonists into the Royal Navy, and many other items caused grave objections from the Americans and sometimes even led to rioting.

There were, of course, corresponding frustrations experienced by the British. There were incidents which caused the mother country to despair in the course of the long years of partnership in warfare. Colonial responses to requests for joint ventures often seemed lethargic, half-hearted; continued pleas for unified action among the colonists seemed to bring no improvement in the chaotic patterns resulting from the diversified attitudes of the various colonies toward war measures; the quality of the colonial militiaman as a fighting soldier—these, and again, many more incidents and situations form the other part of the story. The historian who attempts to analyze actions must step warily among the evidence remaining from those times, especially remembering that it is far easier for the scholar of today to understand and appreciate British policy decisions and actions than it was for the eighteenth-century American colonist, who lacked the information and perhaps the perspective to view the conflicts in their over-all dangers and opportunities.

THE COLONIES AND WAR

In reviewing the history of *The Colonial Wars: 1689–1762* (1964), Howard H. Peckham has pointed out that events during the first of those conflicts, King William's War, had demonstrated flaws in the imperial theories regarding the responsibility for defense of the Empire. England had committed herself in only a limited fashion in that conflict, as regards the American theater of operations. She had dispatched only four companies of soldiers to America, relying upon the colonists to devise their own defense and whatever aggressive, offensive operations they might arrange against the French. The result of this, in Peckham's view, was that the colonists learned an awareness of the need to provide for their own defense, an awareness that might have been reluctantly accepted, but nonetheless became a part of colonial thought. On the other hand, on the basis of the colonists' record, the British concluded that the colonies could easily marshal the necessary men and equipment both to defend themselves and to conquer French Canada, if only they would stop bickering amongst themselves and forget their fears about the royal prerogative. These concepts, says Peckham, to some extent would continue as vehicles for misunderstanding, marring harmonious imperial relationships until the Peace of Paris in 1763.

On the other hand, Peckham also sees concepts of mutual interest developing at an early time in the series of international wars. For example, he believes that, in the northern American provinces, the belief that frontier security could be permanently maintained only by pushing the French off the continent took root from the time of the earliest conflict and, while slowly nurtured, ". . . in two generations this tantalizing hope would mature to a widespread and passionate conviction . . ." among Americans. At the same time, he believes that the first experience in imperial warfare demonstrated to the colonists the benefits possible from intercolonial co-operation, for ". . . although the joint military effort had failed, at least there had been official discussions. The participants were dimly aware that they had certain common problems, such as defense, and that the burden of the solutions might be lightened by some sort of joint action."

These statements by Peckham introduce three topics of major interest to historians—the ability (or willingness) of the Americans to provide for their own defense; the attitude of the American colonists toward the imperial conflicts; and the impetus which military matters brought to the problems of intercolonial co-operation and possible union.

Daniel Boorstin, in the concluding sections of his provocative book *The Americans: The Colonial Experience,* comments on the first of these topics—the willingness of the American colonists to enter into the imperial conflicts. He characterizes the performance of the American colonists during the Great War for Empire as a record of generally small and grudging contributions. He sees the British burden proportionately greater than that of the colonists, and explains the reluctance of the

Americans to co-operate fully in the war partly as a result of the long-endured necessity of the colonists to provide for their own defense against Indian threats. Life in wilderness America, explains Boorstin, required the maintenance and exercise of arms on an individual (family) basis. Accustomed to that state of personal defense, the colonist believed that local (community) defense was a necessity and contributed to it for his own personal protection. But warfare of an offensive nature, against colonial possessions of Spain or France, involved other theories and other practices. It necessitated commitments of manpower outside provincial boundaries, leaving the "homeland" of the colonist open and undefended. This led to a serious hesitation on the part of the colonies to provide requested men and supplies and to the failure of colonies to co-operate with each other in military matters.

Moreover, even when commitments were forthcoming, Boorstin believes that the American colonist recorded a rather dismal record as a soldier, citing the 1745 capture of Louisbourg as the only instance of a successful, provincial, large-scale military operation. Even that he ascribes to "lucky coincidence" rather than successful military strategy. He asserts that colonial troops were ill-trained, lacking in order and neatness, undisciplined, living a "free and easy" life under the command of elected officers. They could not be counted on in actual battle and in the end military victories against France and Spain were possible only by fielding a professional British army in America.

Not only did the American colonists follow their own ideas about military defense; Boorstin also explains that the Americans' reluctance in warfare resulted from their lack of interest in wars fought for conquest or expansion of the Empire. The American was not even interested in such obvious objectives as the reduction of French control in Canada. Boorstin asserts that the ordinary provincial American, be he either a western pioneer who was concerned with his own protection against the "local" danger, or the more secure American colonist on the seaboard, was not moved by concepts of expanding empires or opening new areas for British control. He was, says Boorstin, much more interested in keeping the New World out of European power politics. In effect, the Americans were already isolationists.

Boorstin's characterization of the Americans as uninterested in European diplomacy, desirous of pursuing parochial, isolated interests, is challenged by other scholars. Howard H. Peckham, as indicated above, argues the opposite was true, claiming that the Americans came to accept the doctrine of the elimination of the French from North America as essential to their security. Max Savelle and Robert Middlekauff (*A History of Colonial America,* 1964) contend that, rather than being "pawns" of European diplomacy, the colonists were as anxious for wars of expansion as their British cousins, for the Americans, no less than the British, equated war with Empire and "Empire meant profit."

Lawrence Henry Gipson, who has studied the events of the years of the Great War for Empire in more detail than any other single scholar, in the sixth volume of *The British Empire before the American Revolution,* explains why historians have misunderstood the colonists' reactions to the imperial struggles. Gipson believes that modern historians too often view the events of those war years through the eyes of the propagandists for the American Revolution, particularly through the writings of Thomas Paine. In his *Common Sense* Paine painted a picture of independence creating an isolated, secure America, free from dangers of being "dragged into" unnecessary and unwanted warfare by Britain. To make the dream purer, Paine suggested that the colonists had never really had any interest in the warfare of the last three-quarters of a century; they had become engulfed in those wars only because they were a part of the British Empire. But it was Englishmen who had reaped the advantages, said Paine, leaving the colonists to pay a disproportionate share in money, material, and human lives.

Gipson believes that Paine has misled historians like George Bancroft and others into a wrong assessment of the colonists' role in the international struggle for empire in North America. He questions ". . . whether any responsible American in any of the colonies could have been found during the years between 1750 and 1760 who would have subscribed to Paine's beliefs." Gipson cites requests from the colonists for military aid; he asserts that it was France, not England, who began the troubles by sending an armed force into the Ohio Country. Once begun, the war was continued by colonists who quickly looked to England for aid in winning the western area. Britain then faced a choice. She could pursue a narrow policy, calculate the cost of trading losses as the Dutch presumably had done in the seventeenth century, and if the colonies were not worth their rescue, could have refused aid. Or rejecting this, Britain could have, and did, make her decision on the basis of newer, eighteenth-century concepts of colonialism—concepts which involved full protection and security for all parts of the Empire.

The decision made, Britain proceeded to fight for retention of the Ohio Valley, making the North American theater (especially during the energetic and capable leadership of William Pitt) the principal arena of the entire conflict. The victory of British arms on the Plains of Abraham above Quebec City in 1759 is counted one of the decisive battles of the modern world, for it sealed the future of the French American empire and marked the high point of Britain's quest for mastery over her long-time rival. That war also brought significant internal changes to Britain's overseas Empire. It provided the occasion for serious consideration of the need for intercolonial co-operation; it led to the appointment of a supreme commander of forces in North America for the first time in the history of the Empire.

Military matters were not the only elements working toward the idea of imperial unification in the mid-eighteenth century. The earlier imperialists' concern with uniformity had never been completely forgotten, and from time to time suggestions for consolidating controls in the interests of improving regulation of the Indian trade or commercial and industrial regulations were made. But, in the eighteenth century, military problems of the Empire were most often responsible for generating interest in the possibility of intercolonial union.

Some minor modifications had been instituted. For example, the royal governors of New York and Massachusetts had been given military supervision over the neighboring corporate colonies of Connecticut and Rhode Island. But larger plans were never carried to fruition. In 1721, motivated by experiences in the early wars, the Board of Trade put together a blueprint for unified control, calling for the appointment of a single officer who would serve as the King's principal agent in America. His authority would allow him to co-ordinate colonial military efforts in raising men and money. But the plan had never been effected; no such officer had been appointed.

In 1754, on the eve of the Great War for Empire, the Board of Trade returned to the question of more consolidated control in the colonies, proceeding to frame a plan of union. And the threat of that war led to the summoning of the Albany Conference in America, to consider Indian, defense, and military problems and possibilities of greater colonial co-operation. The Albany Conference, of course, went far beyond the immediate war threat in drafting a plan of union, offering a scheme which would have erected a general, dominion-like status for the American provinces. That plan proved unacceptable to both Britain and to the individual colonies in America. And the Board of Trade's scheme never became more than a "paper plan."

Nonetheless, when war actually erupted and the British decided to field an army in the New World, General Edward Braddock was commissioned the first over-all commander of military forces in British North America. The creation of a commander-in-chief for the American Empire was only one of the many changes in imperial relationships occasioned by the last of the intercolonial wars. The increasing emphasis the war focused upon the American colonies exposed American problems and situations to many Englishmen. Conversely, the presence of British military forces in such large numbers provided opportunities for colonists to view at close range the inner workings of the British army. Imperial relationships would never be the same after the war ended as they had been before, for Britain and America now knew each other more intimately than they had at any earlier time. And out of those circumstances would come motivations for imperial changes.

Matters of defense were not the only issues involved. Additional concern arose over the colonial trade with enemy Caribbean islands and Britain's attempts to halt that trade, leading to suggestions for revising basic imperial structures which dated back to the Cromwellian years. Indian policy, land policy, ecclesiastical affairs, as well as such cost-accounting elements as revenue receipts and military expenditures, would provide the ingredients for the fashioning of new and radically different policies in the post-war "reconstruction" of the Empire. The story of those changes, and the colonists' reactions to them, is another story—the story of the coming of the American Revolution.

A SUMMING UP

By 1763 the British Empire was at least a century old. Created in the middle years of the seventeenth century, it had been the offspring of mixed parentage, conceived to meet demands and desires of a rising group of English merchants, a revenue-seeking Crown, a landed gentry interested in expansion of its income from the New World, and a group of committed "imperialists" who saw the nation's interests furthered by expansion of overseas enterprises. There had always tended to be two empires. There was the theoretical Empire, existing in the minds of some English statesmen and politicians, as well as in the minds of some American colonists; an Empire in which the center (that is, the homeland) arranged the constitutional, political, economic, strategic, and other affairs for the imperial world. But there was another Empire—the real, working Empire, which compromises, inefficiency, inattention, and ignorance had allowed to develop and within which the American colonists played a more dynamic, more substantial role in policy making. How separate and distinct those two empires had become began to be revealed in the last years of the old colonial system.

Economically, the Empire had been a success. British commerce and industry had grown, and colonial commerce and industry had kept pace. The jealousies and fears of the rest of Europe directed toward Britain in the eighteenth century was proof of the success of the British economic empire. Historians seem now generally agreed that, with a few significant exceptions, the American colonies also prospered economically under the old colonial system.

Britain also created opportunities for political advancement in the colonies, although much of what took place occurred in spite of, not because of, imperial policies. The basic decisions and assumptions of the seventeenth century regarding local participation in political affairs, so different from the structure of New Spain or New France, allowed the rise of the representative assemblies, the agencies that were to become the most distinctive and, in many ways, the single most important political agencies in the American colonies. But other historical developments, as in the office of the royal governors, also modified the theoretical nature of imperial relationships and afforded opportunities for self-expression by the American colonists.

The British Empire at times was wracked with the problems common to all "federal" organizations; centralizing and decentralizing forces collided to produce frictions. Whether such moments should be considered "normal" and a state of "perpetual discordance" the true tenor of the Empire, or whether the collisions and frictions were minor set against the more imposing theme of harmony within the Empire, historians do not, and perhaps never will, agree. But unquestionably the situations were complicated by the fact that time did not stand still. Colonial society underwent constant change, with accompanying stresses, during the century of imperial rule. With clashes between various groups in the colonies occurring, it was perhaps inevitable that some groups within the colonies would shape their policies to encompass co-operation with imperial agencies while others, embarking in the opposite direction, would use anti-imperial sentiments to enhance their local following.

Out of the varied experiences of these years, the American people gained the heritage that would define their nation in the decades and centuries to follow. The British Empire had offered them priceless opportunities to learn the arts of self-government, to cultivate in a relatively unrestricted way social controls and economic opportunities more relaxed than had been known in the past. Easy acquisition of land, relatively free immigration, religious toleration created by necessity if not conviction, a fluid social structure in which individual attainment (ordinarily economic) rather than bloodlines counted —these were the distinctive features of the American colonial society. They would also become distinctive characteristics of the American nation.

Bibliographical Essay

The literature describing the relationships between the American colonies and the British Empire is voluminous, but the more general evaluations are older works; recent assessments tend to be fragmentary in nature, devoted to analysis of particular aspects of those relationships. Perhaps the most useful introductory statements are to be found in the appropriate sections or chapters of the recent general textbooks in American colonial history. Of these, Clarence Ver Steeg's *The Formative Years, 1607–1763* (New York, 1964) deserves first mention, because within a relatively brief book Ver Steeg presents both current interpretations on a variety of topics and his own evaluations on others. His book contains a bibliographical essay with excellent annotations. David Hawke's *The Colonial Experience* (Indianapolis, 1966) is a more detailed statement of colonial history, with some of the same virtues. A third general text is Max Savelle and Robert Middlekauff, *A History of Colonial America*, rev. ed. (New York, 1964).

Moving from the general textbooks to the scholarly statements resting on research in primary sources, Klaus E. Knorr, *British Colonial Theories, 1570–1850* (Toronto, 1944), provides a detailed introduction to the thoughts and interests responsible for the creation of the first British Empire. From that it is a natural step to the classical statements of the early twentieth-century "imperial" historians whose major works still constitute the most detailed, general accounts of imperial relationships. Charles M. Andrews' great work, *The Colonial Period of American History* (4 vols.; New Haven, 1934–1937),* ranks first, with particular attention directed to the fourth volume, entitled *England's Commercial and Colonial Policy*. Less useful as an introduction because of their great detail, the works of Herbert L. Osgood, *The American Colonies in the Seventeenth Century* (3 vols.; New York, 1904–1907), and *The American Colonies in the Eighteenth Century* (4 vols.; New York, 1924), might be consulted on specific questions. The third member, with Andrews and Osgood, of the founding triumvirate of the "imperial school," George L. Beer, presented his findings in *The Origins of the British Colonial System, 1578–1660* (New York, 1908); *The Old Colonial System* (2 vols.; New York, 1912); and *British Colonial Policy, 1754–1765* (New York, 1907).

These historians' general sympathy with Britain in her problems of imperial control, and their tendency to ignore or de-emphasize internal colonial problems, have led to modern re-appraisals of colonial-imperial relationships. Thus far, these re-evaluations have been largely restricted to examination of specific aspects of, or episodes concerning, imperial affairs. Exceptions are the appropriate chapters of the well-balanced survey of *The Southern Colonies in the Seventeenth Century* by Wesley F. Craven, the first volume in the "History of the South" series (Baton Rouge, 1949). Craven's book is nearer contemporary historical thought although, even here, there are specific interpretive problems for which more recent evaluations are available. An illustration is provided in the matter of Bacon's Rebellion. Craven provides a reasonable corrective to Thomas J. Wertenbaker's earlier *Torchbearer of the Revolution* (Princeton, 1940), but the student will want to compare it with the more recent work by Wilcomb E. Washburn, *The Governor and the Rebel* (Chapel Hill, 1957).

There is no single volume comparable to Craven's for the northern colonies in British America during the years when the

* Titles marked with an asterisk (*) are available in paperback editions.

Empire was being created. The story must be put together from a variety of publications, including studies by Bernard Bailyn, *The New England Merchants in the Seventeenth Century* (Cambridge, 1955)* and Michael G. Hall, *Edward Randolph and the American Colonies* (Chapel Hill, 1960). Both of these scholars balance imperial and colonial affairs in judicious manner. Recent interpretations of the events of the Glorious Revolution are indicated in the editors' introductions in the documentary collection *The Glorious Revolution in America* (Chapel Hill, 1964),* edited by Michael G. Hall, Lawrence H. Leder, and Michael G. Kammen. Leder has added further appraisals in *Robert Livingston and the Politics of Colonial New York, 1654–1728* (Chapel Hill, 1961). This is a fine case study of provincial politics and imperial relationships extending into the years after 1689.

As suggested in the second chapter of this book, a reader embarking upon a search for modern evaluations of the economic aspects of the imperial connection upon the American colonies might well begin with Oliver M. Dickerson's *The Navigation Acts and the American Revolution* (Philadelphia, 1951).* Although Dickerson is concerned with the pre-Revolutionary years, the first half of his book provides the most recent general assessment of the effects of the mercantile system upon colonial economic development. Dickerson's assertions of beneficial effects from the imperial connection are too unqualified to satisfy some scholars, and the reader might balance Dickerson's views by examining Lawrence A. Harper, *The English Navigation Laws* (New York, 1939), and an essay by Harper, "The Effect of the Navigation Acts on the Thirteen Colonies," in Richard B. Morris (ed.), *The Era of the American Revolution* (New York, 1939).* Besides Harper's studies, additional qualifications may be found in Curtis P. Nettels, "British Mercantilism and the Economic Development of the Thirteen Colonies," *The Journal of Economic History,* XII (Spring 1952), 105–14. The same author's classic study of the interrelationships between currency and commerce is *The Money Supply in the American Colonies before 1720* (Madison, 1934).

More specific attention is devoted to particular aspects of economic regulation in Gilman M. Ostrander, "The Colonial Molasses Trade," *Agricultural History,* XXX (April 1956), 77–84; the first part of Victor S. Clark, *History of Manufactures in the United States,* rev. ed. (3 vols.; New York, 1929); Arthur C. Bining, *British Regulation of the Colonial Iron Industry* (Philadelphia,

1933); and in Joseph J. Malone, *Pine Trees and Politics: The Naval Stores and Forest Policy in Colonial New England* (Seattle, 1964). Stuart Bruchey has included some documents relative to imperial regulation in *The Colonial Merchant: Sources and Readings* (New York, 1966).*

A fine introduction to the constitutional and political aspects of colonial-imperial relationships is Leonard W. Labaree, *Royal Government in America: A Study of the British Colonial System before 1783* (New Haven, 1930). Labaree's work will probably prove more useful than the generally non-interpretive volume by Arthur B. Keith, *Constitutional History of the First British Empire* (London, 1930). Specific studies of the individual agencies of imperial control are numerous, but few of them include analysis of the effects of regulation upon the colonies. Among the best are the older study by Oliver M. Dickerson, *American Colonial Government* (Cleveland, 1912), which is a study of the Board of Trade, and the more recent works by Dora M. Clark, *The Rise of the British Treasury* (New Haven, 1960), and Thomas C. Barrow, *Trade and Empire: The British Customs Service in Colonial America* (Cambridge, 1967).

There is no modern, general account of the office of royal governor, but the careers of individual governors have been detailed by John A. Schutz in *William Shirley: King's Governor of Massachusetts* (Chapel Hill, 1961), and in *Thomas Pownall: British Defender of American Liberty* (Glendale, Calif., 1951). Additional assessments of the office are contained in William W. Abbot, *The Royal Governors of Georgia, 1754–1775* (Chapel Hill, 1959). Jack P. Greene, in *The Quest for Power: The Lower House of Assembly in the Southern Royal Colonies, 1689–1776* (Chapel Hill, 1963), delineates with care the various aspects of the elected assemblies' rise in real power during the eighteenth century.

Some of the works already mentioned contain evaluations of colonial political practices, but the "case" for a democratic colonial structure is best championed by Robert E. Brown in *Middle-Class Democracy and the Revolution in Massachusetts, 1691–1780* (Ithaca, N.Y., 1955), and Robert E. Brown and B. Katherine Brown, *Virginia, 1705–1786: Democracy or Aristocracy?* (East Lansing, Mich., 1964). Among the writings of those who view colonial society as less democratic, Merrill Jensen's article, "Democracy and the American Revolution," *Huntington Library Quarterly,* XX (August 1957), 321–41, is representative.

The military and strategic aspects of the imperial connection may be studied from a variety of works, although we need more general evaluations incorporating the significant findings of monographic studies. Howard H. Peckham, *The Colonial Wars, 1689–1762* (Chicago, 1964),* furnishes essential data, but is somewhat disappointing because of the general lack of interpretive analysis. It might be used in conjunction with the first chapter of John Shy, *Toward Lexington: The Role of the British Army in the Coming of the Revolution* (Princeton, 1965), in which the author discusses both imperial theory and practice in military matters. A specific study, detailing some aspects of interrelationships between colonies and Empire during Queen Anne's War is George M. Waller, *Samuel Vetch: Colonial Enterpriser* (Chapel Hill, 1960).

The American colonists' response to imperial warfare is analyzed in the concluding part ("Warfare and Diplomacy") of Daniel J. Boorstin, *The Americans: The Colonial Experience* (New York, 1958),* a provocative volume which contains, in its earlier sections, analyses of other aspects of colonial society. Boorstin's description of colonial military affairs is quite different from the assessment of others, who see the Americans as being as aggressive and expansionistic as the British. This view is reflected in Max Savelle, "The American Balance of Power and European Diplomacy, 1713–1778" in the above-cited Morris (ed.), *The Era of the American Revolution.** Savelle's essay is extremely useful in placing imperial-colonial situations within the framework of general European diplomatic developments. In the same book, Clarence E. Carter examines "The Office of Commander in Chief: A Phase of Imperial Unity on the Eve of the Revolution."

Relations between individual colonies and the mother country have been investigated in detail by Winfred R. Root in *The Relations of Pennsylvania with the British Government, 1696–1765* (Philadelphia, 1912) and by Trevor R. Reese in *Colonial Georgia: A Study of British Imperial Policy in the Eighteenth Century* (Athens, Ga., 1963). As Clarence Ver Steeg has noted, we need similar studies of other colonies.

The reader desiring selected source materials, in addition to the works of historians, will want to examine *American Colonial Documents to 1776,* edited by Merrill Jensen. This carefully selected volume of documents, complete with introductions and bibliographical notations, is Volume 9 of the Oxford University Press series,

"English Historical Documents," David D. Douglas, general editor (London, 1953 to date).

Finally, transcending in scope any of the separate categories indicated above, but helpful for understanding the history of any of them as related to the years from 1750 until the close of the colonial era, is the unique work by Lawrence H. Gipson under the general title *The British Empire before the American Revolution* (New York, 1936 to date). In the twelve volumes published thus far may be found the most remarkable achievement of a single colonial scholar in recent times.

INDEX